Dear Lisa & Bri
    Mrs Fish &

wish every Blessing for you
new home. together with the
prayer that God will prosper
your Christian work and witness
together across many years.

    Thank you for asking
me to have a part in officiating
at your wedding.

    To you and yours —
Always — the very first

    most Cordially yours

    [signature]

    Pastor

WHOM GOD HATH JOINED
Revised Edition

WHOM GOD HATH JOINED

Revised Edition

by
DAVID R. MACE

THE WESTMINSTER PRESS
PHILADELPHIA

© THE EPWORTH PRESS 1953, 1973

PUBLISHED BY THE WESTMINSTER PRESS ®
PHILADELPHIA, PENNSYLVANIA

PRINTED IN THE UNITED STATES OF AMERICA

Library of Congress Cataloging in Publication Data

Mace, David Robert.
  Whom God hath joined.

  Bibliography: p.
  1. Marriage. I. Title.
HQ734.M1845 1973   301.42′7   73-8871
ISBN 0-664-20988-2

ACKNOWLEDGMENTS

I AM glad to express my indebtedness to the following authors and their publishers for the use of extracts from copyright works:

Padwick, Constance E., *Temple Gairdner of Cairo*, S.P.C.K., London, 1929;

Bottome, Phyllis, *And So We Got Married*, Blandford Press Ltd., London, 1951;

Blanco White, Mrs. Amber, *Worry in Women*, Gollancz, London, 1941;

Carpenter, Edward, *Love's Coming of Age*, George Allen & Unwin, Ltd., London, 1930;

Maurois, André, *The Art of Living*, English Universities Press, Ltd., London;

Griffith, Edward F., *Morals in the Melting Pot*, Gollancz, London, 1938;

Wayne, T. G., *Morals and Marriage*, Longmans, Green & Co., London, 1936;

Mersch, E., *Love, Marriage and Chastity*, Sheed & Ward, London;

Hutchinson, E. D., *Creative Sex*, George Allen & Unwin, Ltd., London, 1936;

Ellis, Havelock, 'On Life and Sex': *Little Essays of Love and Virtue*, Wm. Heinemann (Medical Books) Ltd., London;

McDougall, William, *Character and the Conduct of Life*, Methuen & Co. Ltd., London, 1927;

Gallichan, Walter M., *The Psychology of Marriage*, T. Werner Laurie, Ltd., London;

Bridge, Ann, *Four-Part Setting*, Chatto & Windus, London;

Jung, C. G., *Contributions to Analytical Psychology*, Routledge & Kegan Paul, Ltd., London;

Dorner, I. A., *System of Christian Ethics*, T. & T. Clark, Edinburgh;

Grubb, Norman P., *C. T. Studd*, Lutterworth Press, London;

Gibran, Kahlil, *The Prophet*, Wm. Heinemann, Ltd., London;

von Haering, Theodor, *The Ethics of the Christian Life*, G. P. Putnam's Sons, New York, 1909;

Younghusband, Sir Francis, *Modern Mystics*, John Murray, Ltd., London, 1935;

How, the Rt. Rev. John, *The Venture of Christian Marriage*, G.F.S., London;

Hughes, M. V., *A London Family*, O.U.P., London, 1946;

Keyserling, Count Hermann, *The Book of Marriage*, Jonathan Cape, Ltd., London. (Quotations from *Marriage as a Task*, by Alfred Adler, and *Marriage in the New World* by Beatrice M. Hinkle.)

Russell, Bertrand, *The Conquest of Happiness*, George Allen & Unwin, Ltd., London;

Lofthouse, W. F., *Ethics and the Family*, Hodder & Stoughton, Ltd., London, 1912;

Macaulay, Mary, *The Art of Marriage*, Delisle, Ltd., London, 1952;

Bailey, Derrick Sherwin, *The Mystery of Love and Marriage*, S.C.M. Press, Ltd., London, 1952;

Henson, H. Hensley, *Christian Marriage*, Cassell & Co. Ltd., London, 1907.

D. M.

CONTENTS

Page

Preface to the Revised Edition xi

Part 1. THE PURPOSE OF MARRIAGE

1. *The Divine Institution.* 13
2. *The First Object of Marriage—Procreation* . . 15
3. *The Second Object of Marriage—Sexual Fulfilment* . 18
4. *The Third Object of Marriage—Comradeship* . . 20
5. *The First Standard—Monogamy* 23
6. *The Second Standard—Fidelity* 26
7. *The Third Standard—Life-Long Union* . . . 29

Part 2. THE INTIMACIES OF MARRIAGE

1. *Belonging to One Another* 33
2. *The Blessing of Sexual Union* 35
3. *Meeting Each Other's Needs.* 39
4. *When Two Become One* 41
5. *Attaining Sexual Harmony* 45
6. *Planned Parenthood* 48
7. *The Sacrament of Love* 51

Part 3. THE FELLOWSHIP OF MARRIAGE

1. *Meant for Each Other.* 55
2. *The Shared Life.* 57
3. *The Partnership of Equals* 60
4. *Masculine and Feminine* 63
5. *The Continuous Task of Mutual Adjustment* . . 65
6. *Times of Testing* 68
7. *The Spiritual Pilgrimage* 71

Part 4. THE WIDER IMPLICATIONS OF MARRIAGE

Page

1. *Getting On with In-Laws* 75
2. *Friends and Neighbours* 77
3. *Sharing in the World's Work* 80
4. *Church Loyalty* 83
5. *The Task of Parenthood* 86
6. *Family Relationships* 88
7. *The Christian Home* 91

APPENDIX

Books Recommended for Further Reading . . . 94

PREFACE TO THE REVISED EDITION

IT was in the Summer of 1952, in a secluded cottage in Bedfordshire, that I wrote the first version of this little book. I recall it as a very happy experience. My wife Vera worked at it with me, reading over each section as I completed it, and helping me in a wide search for suitable quotations. It was thus a united labour of love. Deeply thankful for our own very happy marriage, we tried to offer reliable guidelines to young couples starting out together.

Since then, twenty years have passed, and the book—separately published in British and American editions—has been widely read throughout the English-speaking world, and even translated into other languages. Tens of thousands of copies have been given to engaged couples by their parents, by ministers of religion, or by interested friends. Some of these couples have written to tell me how much it helped them in their early days of married life. Other couples have described how, following a marriage crisis, the reading of the book led them to a happy reconciliation. One American couple were living apart, with divorce proceedings already started, when their minister gave them a copy and exacted a promise that they would read it. A few days later they called off the divorce and re-established their home.

These events have more than fulfilled my highest hopes for the book; and I am glad to know that yet another edition is now to be printed. I have taken advantage of this opportunity not only to rewrite this Preface, but also to go through the book and make a few needful changes; and to provide a new and up-to-date list of books for further reading.

The book can of course be read right through, as one would read any other volume. But it will be noticed that I have arranged the material with an alternative use in mind. By dividing it up into four parts, and then further dividing each part into seven sections, it has been possible to provide a series of daily readings for a month. The sections begin with appropriate quotations from the Bible, from various forms of the Marriage Service, and from other sources.

My hope is that some married couples, and some couples looking toward marriage, will read the book together. They could do this by taking it in turns to read aloud; or by going through it separately and discussing what they have read. In this way they could devote one month to a serious consideration of what their marriage means to them. The best time of all to do this might be the first month of married life. But any time—not least a time of difficulty in the relationship—will do. Each reading ends with a simple prayer, which might be followed by the Lord's Prayer repeated together.

DAVID R. MACE

Part 1

THE PURPOSE OF MARRIAGE

1. *The Divine Institution*

So God created man in his own image, in the image of God created
he him; male and female created he them. And God blessed them.

GENESIS 1²⁷⁻⁸

It is fit, therefore, that we bear in mind that marriage is ordained of
God as the sacrament of human society. It was hallowed by our Lord,
both by His presence and by His solemn words. It is commended in
the Christian Scriptures as honourable in all who engage in it not
inadvisedly or lightly, but reverently and discreetly, and in the fear of
God. And it has been consecrated by the faithful keeping of good
men and good women in every generation.

Into this holy estate these two persons come now to be joined
together.

THE MARRIAGE SERVICE—CONGREGATIONAL VERSION

Your letter arrived this afternoon: I got it at five o'clock, and put it
unopened in my pocket, got on my bicycle and rode out into the
country. I felt I must read it alone and with God. I will show you the
place one day. Then I raised my heart in prayer to God, as I have been
doing many times each day since the day at Brindisi. I had utterly
committed the whole matter to Him. . . . In the quiet light of the
setting sun, I broke the seal and saw the Yes. I bowed my head and
took you from the hands of God: then gave yourself and myself back
to Him to fulfil His utter will. . . . Please God these things will make
something heavenly, something spiritual and ethereal in our relations
one to another. Something that God may have pleasure in and use to
His own glory.

TEMPLE GAIRDNER OF CAIRO, in a letter to his future wife

WHEN two people start their married life they are naturally
not thinking of much except the joy and delight which they
have in one another. The long time of waiting (and for all

lovers it seems long, whether it is days or years) is over at last. They now belong completely to one another, in the sight of God and with the full blessing of all their friends. The happiness and fulfilment they experience at this time will never be quite equalled again. Edward Wilson of the Antarctic wrote to his friend Fraser at the time of his marriage and said, 'I am as happy as it is given to mortals ever to be on this earth'.

Yet sooner or later all husbands and wives must consider marriage not just as a personal experience, but as a social institution. We have to decide what we believe about marriage in general, as well as what we feel about our own marriage in particular.

When you try to do this you will find that there are two ways of looking at marriage. First, it is a human institution, found in one form or another all over the world. Edward Westermarck, the great anthropologist, came to the conclusion that marriage is an essential part of the life of all settled communities, ancient or modern. Even in the animal world, lasting partnerships are formed between male and female which sometimes continue for life.

So the very private and personal bliss you share as husband and wife links you with a vast company, stretching back to remote ages and out to the ends of the earth. Countless millions of married couples have held each other's hands and looked into each other's eyes, have breathed mutual assurances of love into each other's ears in languages old and new. With the tireless march of the passing years, each new generation enters into this great heritage.

There is another way of looking at marriage—as a divine institution. The Bible begins by telling us that God chose to make the human race in the form of individuals of two different kinds, so that they might meet and love and marry and complete each other. And on all this God looked with satisfaction and blessed it. Generations of Christian men and women have interpreted their love for one another as a gift from the God of love; and this has made it seem even more wonderful and sacred than it could otherwise have been.

Those of us who choose to be married according to the Christian faith and by a Christian minister join ourselves to this happy company of 'good men and good women in every generation'. Those faithful couples who stretch back in an unbroken line for nearly two thousand years have now committed the honour of Christian marriage into our keeping. When we think of this, we will want to pray, as Temple Gairdner did, that we may be worthy of so great a trust.

PRAYER

O Thou who in Thy great wisdom hast chosen to make us incomplete without each other, and hast given us to each other to love and to cherish; enable us to make of our marriage a thing of such beauty and joy that it may fulfil all our hopes and dreams. And may our fellowship together be worthy of the great heritage into which we are now privileged to enter. Amen.

2. *The First Object of Marriage—Procreation*

Male and female created he them. And God said unto them, Be fruitful, and multiply, and replenish the earth.

GENESIS 1^{27-8}

Duly considering the causes for which Matrimony was ordained. . . . First, it was ordained for the increase of mankind according to the will of God, and that children might be brought up in the fear and nurture of the Lord, and to the praise of His Holy Name.

THE MARRIAGE SERVICE

Lovers radiate well-being. They seem to take a practical and tingling pleasure in increasing each other's joy. Nature is always on the side of lovers. But she makes no bones about her purpose. Nature gives men and women this overwhelming desire, dowered with beauty and delight, in order to produce children.

PHYLLIS BOTTOME—*And So We Got Married*

The achievement of a deep and abiding love between a husband and wife normally results in the growing desire to share, as well as to perpetuate, their happiness. The natural way to do this is by raising a family of happy, intelligent, healthy, emotionally mature children. The result is probably life's superlative satisfaction.

F. ALEXANDER MAGOUN—*Love and Marriage*

MOST forms of the Marriage Service begin with a statement, read by the minister to the couple and congregation, of the three great causes for which matrimony was ordained. In this and the next two sections we shall think of these objects of marriage.

The first end of marriage is to enable children to be born under the best possible conditions, so that they have the loving care of a father and a mother who will work together, and if necessary sacrifice, for their highest good.

Nowadays we have achieved so much control over nature that we tend to think of parenthood as almost a by-product of marriage, something which grows out of the relationship of husband and wife. Yet if we take the long view, it is rather marriage which is a by-product of parenthood. Marriage became necessary, at some far-away point in our misty past, because the human child could not reach his full development without the co-operation and care of two parents. This is as true today as it ever was. One of Edward Westermarck's most profound sayings was: 'Marriage is rooted in the family, and not the family in marriage.'

This might be put a little differently by saying that parents exist to serve their children, not children to serve their parents. It is a fundamental law of life that the older generation must be

willing to sacrifice its interests to those of the younger generation. That law is defied by some people; but only at the risk of
unsettling the foundations of human society.

So the love which draws a man and a woman into marriage
has in it a creative quality and also a sacrificial quality. The
power of fruitfulness which God gave to man is sometimes
called 'procreation'. That word means 'creation for and on
behalf of' another—and the other is God Himself. The
Christian way of thinking about parenthood is that it is a sharing by men and women of the work of the Creator. Just as
God in the beginning made the world of living things, so man
and woman—not separately, but together—have been
appointed God's agents to continue His creative work.

It is right and natural, therefore, that the love of husband
and wife for each other should overflow into a shared love for
a child of their own flesh and blood. This experience brings
new responsibilities and duties—the married pair will have to
unclasp one hand each to bring another into the circle. But
it also brings out new qualities in them both—a depth and
intensity of devotion which makes them ready and willing to
sacrifice and suffer and even die for the sake of their little ones.

Marriage, therefore, is not an end in itself. It is a united
ministry to others. For most couples the first of those others
are their own children. No service which Christian men and
women undertake is more important than this great ministry
of parenthood.

PRAYER

*When we consider the confidence which Thou hast placed in us, O
God, by making us partners of Thy great work of creation, we are
humbled at the thought of our unworthiness. If the blessing of
children should be ours, may it be for us an experience of deep and
lasting joy; and help us to be ready for whatever service or sacrifice it
may require of us. Amen.*

3. *The Second Object of Marriage—Sexual Fulfilment*

And the man said, This is now bone of my bones, and flesh of my flesh. Therefore shall a man cleave unto his wife; and they shall be one flesh. And they were both naked, the man and his wife, and were not ashamed.

GENESIS 2^{23-5}

Duly considering the causes for which Matrimony was ordained. . . . Second, it was ordained in order that the natural instincts and affections, implanted by God, should be hallowed and directed aright; that those who are called of God to this holy estate should continue therein in pureness of living.

THE MARRIAGE SERVICE—REVISED PRAYER BOOK VERSION

The highest and most intimate of spiritual friendships can never be marriage without the union of the flesh: but where the man and woman are one flesh, their indefinite yearnings are replaced by the peacefulness of a pervading possession, the inward energy corresponding to the outward union. Marriage is thus an ordinance peculiarly human. It is adapted to man's composite nature, which is at once fleshly and spiritual.

OSCAR D. WATKINS—*Holy Matrimony*

Intercourse between two people who love one another should produce not merely pleasure and satisfaction, but confidence, harmony, and self-respect. It should relieve anxiety, lessen guilt, and prevent the formation of hostility. And all these consequences, being felt as a gift from the other partner, should fortify affection. To be indifferent to the physical expression of love, still more to dislike it, or to feel that it is in some way shameful, is neither superior nor virtuous nor refined; it is a symptom of mental illness or maladjustment.

AMBER BLANCO WHITE—*Worry in Women*

ONE of the powerful forces which draws men and women together in marriage is the drive of sexual desire. This is a normal, healthy, God-given impulse. It is also a strong and insistent urge. It has to be so; otherwise the vitally important function of reproduction might be neglected, and the continuing purpose of creation would be defeated.

So we are endowed with an intensity of sexual desire far greater than is strictly necessary to carry on the race. Because of this, sex is an emotional high explosive which can do terrible damage when it gets out of hand. All human communities have found that sexual urges have to be controlled. The best way which has been found is for a man and a woman, in marriage, to form a continuous association in which each seeks to meet the other's sexual needs. Thus the drive of this mighty impulse is channelled in a way which does no harm to other people.

That is a somewhat negative way of putting it. Unfortunately the Church has sometimes been sadly negative about sex. The old version of the Prayer Book even spoke of the second purpose of marriage as 'a remedy against sin'! This is true enough. The sin of misusing sex is one into which it is all too easy to fall—and marriage certainly provides an outlet which lessens the temptation to do so. But this seems a very inadequate way of putting the case for marriage.

So it is. Even the Church has to make progress and find better ways of proclaiming its message. And one of the great advances of Christian thinking in our time is the more positive and wholesome way in which we can now look at sex. We can be thankful that we live in an enlightened age in this respect. In the past, men and women were often made to feel that their sexual nature was something of which they ought to be ashamed.

Sex, as we see it today, is not a regrettable overplus of guilty desire which marriage helps us to dispose of secretly. It is a part of our nature which can be a source of deep fulfilment and rich fruitfulness. Quite apart from the wonderful power which it gives us to create new life, it can be used as the instrument of the most tender spiritual love between husband and wife, to refresh and renew and enrich their whole relationship. In fact, it *must* be used in this way, or it will endanger the security of married life.

In the early days of marriage, husband and wife must learn the great art of expressing their love for each other in this mysterious union of their bodies which can be such a deeply spiritual experience. If they can rejoice in it as a great gift from God, then they have achieved a true Christian attitude to sex.

PRAYER

We thank Thee, O God our Creator, that Thou hast made us as we are. Help us as man and wife that through the mutual fulfilment of our bodies we may achieve true unity of spirit. Amen.

4. The Third Object of Marriage—Comradeship

And the Lord God said, It is not good that the man should be alone; I will make him an help meet for him. And the Lord God made a woman, and brought her unto the man.

GENESIS $2^{18, 22}$

Duly considering the causes for which Matrimony was ordained. . . . Third, It was ordained for the mutual society, help, and comfort, that the one ought to have of the other, both in prosperity and adversity.

THE MARRIAGE SERVICE

A wise man soon grows weary of acting the lover, and treating his wife like a mistress, but wants a reasonable companion and a true friend through every stage of his life. It must therefore be your business to qualify yourself for those offices. . . . The grand affair of your life will be to gain and preserve the friendship and esteem of your husband.

DEAN SWIFT, writing to a bride

I value being alone with my husband; it is a quiet I have not lately enjoyed, and it does seem to me one of the great blessings of life. I have much valued my dear husband's company, and feel it sweet that we can so thoroughly enjoy being together, and that we unite so much in our principles and tasks.

ELIZABETH FRY, in a letter

APART from the sexual attraction which they feel for one another, two people marry because a deep friendship has grown up between them which they find very satisfying. The element of comradeship is a most important one in the marriage relationship. All marriages are not blessed with children. Even if they were, children come and go, leaving the couple alone together again. Parenthood, therefore, may enrich marriage; but it will not sustain marriage. Neither will sex. There is much more in marriage than physical love-making. In the daily living together of husband and wife, amid all the changes and accidents of human life, what will matter most of all is that they are true and trusty friends.

We all need friends. Of all the experiences which men and women can encounter, loneliness is one of the most dreaded. As the Bible says, it is not good that a man, or a woman, should be alone. One of our deepest human needs is the need to love and to be loved.

Of course that need can be satisfied apart from marriage. But the close and intimate life together of husband and wife has always provided the ideal solution for most people. Sharing their resources, their plans, their hopes, the married couple grow into a fellowship of warm affection and mutual trust which becomes more and more precious to them as the years go by. At least, that is what marriage ought to be.

The friendship of husband and wife is particularly rich because they are not fully alike. In the Bible story it was not just that the man needed a companion. In that case another man might have met his need. It was that the man's nature was incomplete in itself until the gift of the woman completed it. Nowadays we can smile at the story of how the woman was made out of the man's rib. Yet this is a symbol of the way in which men and women in love regard each other. When they come together in love they do not feel that they are meeting as strangers. They feel that they have always been part of each other from the beginning and that in coming together they are making each other complete.

So it is only half the truth to say that men and women have been made different. The very nature of their differences is that they require each other in order to be truly happy. Love for each other is kindled in their hearts just as desire for each other is kindled in their bodies.

Sometimes this love blazes for a time with great intensity and then dies out. But at its best it glows like a steady fire through long years and becomes a rich and enduring comradeship. Marriage, by bringing man and woman into a secure and exclusive association, provides the conditions in which this comradeship can come naturally to its full maturity.

We have been thinking of the great ends which marriage serves. As you consider them, you will realize that they are deep and fundamental. They do not vary with the passing of the centuries, with the rise and fall of empires, or with climatic variations or social changes. And they are all bound up in one another. Parenthood normally deepens the married couple's affection and enriches their comradeship. Sex makes possible the coming of children on the one hand and the ecstatic rapture of the love relationship on the other. Good fellowship between husband and wife establishes a stable, happy home for their children, while it makes their sexual union something far more significant than the mere gratification of a recurring physical appetite. The three ends of marriage present a trinity in unity.

We rejoice in the happy fellowship which has been ours since love touched our hearts and awakened us to our kinship with each other. As we travel together the unknown road which lies before us, O God, be Thou our Guide. Enable us, in sharing the joys and sorrows which come to us, to grow daily in mutual love, confidence, and trust. Amen.

5. The First Standard—Monogamy

Let every man of you love his wife as himself, and let the wife reverence her husband.

EPHESIANS 5^{33}

And the man shall say, I N take thee N to my wedded wife ... to love and to cherish. And the woman shall likewise say, I N take thee N to my wedded husband ... to love and to cherish.

THE MARRIAGE SERVICE

Between husband and wife there should be no question as to meum and tuum. All things should be in common between them, without any distinction or means of distinguishing.

MARTIN LUTHER—*Table Talk*

That there should exist one other person in the world towards whom all openness of exchange should establish itself, from whom there should be no concealment; whose body should be as dear to one, in every part, as one's own; with whom there should be no sense of Mine or Thine, in property or possession; into whose mind one's thoughts should naturally flow, as it were to know themselves and receive a new illumination; and between whom and oneself there should be a spontaneous rebound of sympathy in all the joys and sorrows and experiences of life; such is perhaps one of the dearest wishes of the soul.

EDWARD CARPENTER

WE have been thinking about the great purposes which marriage has served in human life. Whether we think of it as a human or as a divine institution, these purposes are the same. All people everywhere would be in general agreement about them.

But marriage has not always followed the same pattern. Indeed, when you study its history you discover that there have been many patterns, bewildering in their variety. Needless to say, they have not all served equally well the purposes for which marriage exists.

So it is not enough for us to say: 'This is what marriage was meant to be. These are the ends which it achieves.' If all marriages worked out that way, without effort on the part of the men and women concerned, we should be spared a great deal of trouble. The sad truth, however, is that in practice many people fail to achieve the clear and simple ideals which we have been considering. They mismanage their relationships; they sink to sub-human levels of behaviour; they make themselves and each other miserable and unhappy.

So we have to go further, and say that there are laws which must be honoured if marriage is to fulfil the purposes it was intended to fulfil. Christian people believe that there is a particular pattern of marriage which is God's intention, and that this means accepting standards which many human communities have not been ready to accept. There are three standards specially, which have always been the foundation of the Christian teaching about marriage.

The first foundation is monogamy. Of course we take it for granted that marriage at its best means the union of one man with one woman. At least, we do so in Christian countries. In some communities, however, even in the modern world, it is possible for a man to take several wives; and the fate of those wives can often be very hard.

The Church has sometimes had to fight a long battle for the

acceptance of the Christian standard of monogamy. In the Old Testament there are plenty of stories about men who married more than one wife. It has not always been easy to insist on monogamous marriage when your opponent could quote you cases of polygamy out of the pages of the Bible itself!

Yet the case for the marriage of one man and one woman is overwhelming. How can married people who really study each other's well-being bring a rival into the intimacy of a relationship so close and personal? When you read the fine account which Edward Carpenter gives of the aspirations of the lover, you realize that a fellowship of that kind must necessarily exclude all but the man and woman concerned.

But monogamy, in the Christian sense, means also that husband and wife must treat each other with due respect, as equals. That is a truth which the Church has not always fully accepted. St. Paul, for example, has been criticized a good deal for appearing to suggest that the wife is inferior to the husband and must be meek and submissive to his imperious will. We must remember that Christianity was a very new religion in St. Paul's time, and that all its practical implications had not yet been worked out. We can excuse Paul more readily than we can some of those who came after him, when there had been time to consider the matter. Yet the idea of the inferiority of the wife has continued even in the Marriage Service, where in the old Prayer Book form the wife promises to 'obey' her husband, while he makes no corresponding promise to her.

That is not a Christian concept. In God's eyes the man and the woman are equally loved and equally honoured. Their functions are different; but as co-operating partners in the marriage relationship they are in every sense equals. It has taken us a long time to grow into the fulness of Christian truth in this matter; but we have arrived at last. It is the privilege and the duty of Christian married couples today to exemplify that truth.

O God our Father, we thank Thee that in our marriage Thou hast called us into a partnership where we both count alike in Thy sight. Help us, in mutual consideration and mutual respect, ever to honour each other as we honour thee. Amen.

6. *The Second Standard—Fidelity*

Ye have heard that it was said, Thou shalt not commit adultery: but I say unto you, that every one that looketh on a woman to lust after her hath committed adultery with her already in his heart.

MATTHEW 5[27-28]

Then shall the minister say unto the man, Wilt thou have this woman to thy wedded wife . . . and forsaking all other, keep thee only unto her, so long as ye both shall live? . . . And unto the woman, Wilt thou have this man to thy wedded husband. . . . and forsaking all other, keep thee only unto him, so long as ye both shall live?

THE MARRIAGE SERVICE

It is a formidable decision to make when one says: 'I bind myself for life: I have chosen: from now on my aim will be, not to search for someone who may please me, but to please the one I have chosen.' Yet this decision can alone produce a successful marriage, and if the vow is not sincere the couple's chances for marriage are very slim, for it will run the risk of disruption, when the first obstacles and the inevitable difficulties of life in common are encountered.

ANDRÉ MAUROIS—*The Art of Living*

IT has always been the Christian teaching that sexual union is a sacramental experience, to be shared only with the beloved mate. This arises naturally out of the standard of monogamy which we have already considered. If the intimate and deeply personal nature of the fellowship between husband and wife excludes the idea of a third partner to the marriage, it also excludes the idea of sharing that intimacy with another person outside the marriage partnership.

The very idea of such a thing is remote from the minds of true lovers. The thought of an act of infidelity fills them with horror. It would violate completely the warm and tender trust which they feel towards each other.

Yet here also the Christian Church has had to fight for its standard. In Old Testament times adultery meant something different from what it means to us today. It meant only a relationship outside marriage in which a married *woman* was involved. A relationship between a married *man* and a woman who was not married was not an offence against the man's wife. So there was a 'double standard' which discriminated between the man and the woman.

Christian teaching has always been clear on this point. Faithfulness is expected equally of the husband and of the wife. The best, the most stable, the most satisfying kind of marriage is that in which the couple think of their intimate life together as a secluded walled garden where no one else ever comes—a little private kingdom apart from the rush and roar of the world's life in which they can enjoy the full and free expression of their mutual love and be refreshed and renewed. To allow an interloper to break into that garden, or a usurper to invade that kingdom, would be to threaten the very heart of the marriage with grave danger, and even with destruction.

The standard of fidelity which Christ set, however, begins not in the realm of action, but in the realm of thought. He understood men and women; and he knew well enough that before there is open unfaithfulness between husband and wife there is nearly always a long period of secret disloyalty which prepares the way for the act of adultery. So he declared that it is here, in the mind, that the Christian must set a continual watch upon himself.

There have been people of fanatical zeal who have distorted this saying of Jesus. He obviously did not mean that a young man seeking a wife should experience no feelings of sexual desire as he contemplated an eligible young woman. Nor did He mean that the wholesome pleasure a man might feel in admiring a beautiful woman, or the delight with which a woman might look upon a fine specimen of manhood, was evil in itself. What He meant, surely, was that the best way in which we can all safeguard ourselves from unfaithfulness is to refuse to let the imagination dwell upon the thought of a sexual relationship which if it actually took place would violate a marriage, our own or another's. There is no doubt that the world would be a much happier place if that standard were more widely accepted. It is certainly our duty as Christian husbands and wives to strive to live up to it. As Thomas Ken put it, we must 'guard the first springs of thought and will'.

Christian husbands and wives make solemn vows of loyalty to each other. The best way to keep those vows is to strive to be completely loyal in *every* area of your relationship. Those who live to please one another, and to trust one another, in the little things, generally find that the big issues take care of themselves.

PRAYER

Keep us faithful all our days, O God, to the vows we made to each other, and to Thee, when we stood together at the altar. Day by day, keep us ever true, in word, thought, and deed. Amen.

7. *The Third Standard—Life-Long Union*

And there came unto him Pharisees, and asked him, Is it lawful for a man to put away his wife?

MARK 10²

MARK 10^2

Then shall they give their troth to each other in this manner. The man, I take thee to be my wedded wife, to have and to hold . . . till death us do part. . . . And the woman likewise, I take thee to be my wedded husband, to have and to hold . . . till death us do part. . . .

THE MARRIAGE SERVICE

> When spirit irresistible
> Grasps and holds within itself
> The elements,
> No angel severeth
> The twin natures thus joined
> In their inmost being.

GOETHE

The ideal that Christ set before people was to marry and accept what came; but I agree with you that He made no law on the subject. It is only in later Christian history that we get the idea of absolute law. Christ always taught that the administration of any law was to be tempered with the idea of God as being merciful and loving.

EDWARD F. GRIFFITH—Morals in the Melting-Pot

MANY Christians have understood the New Testament to mean that marriage is an absolutely binding life-long commitment. The vows in the wedding service can also be interpreted in this way.

However, the principle that marriage is an indissoluble union, an irreversible contract, is no longer accepted today by most people. They reason that couples stumble blindly into the wedding ceremony without careful consideration, even without really knowing each other as persons. Sometimes they are very sincere, and think they are deeply in love. Others will say, quite seriously, 'We just don't know how durable our relationship is. But let's get married, and see how it works. If we don't suit each other, we can always get a divorce'.

Few sincere Christians would be likely to enter marriage in that spirit. The failure of a marriage between Christian people is always a particularly sad event, for themselves and for their friends. To avoid this possibility, Christians have a special obligation to chose their partners wisely and to go into marriage only after careful preparation, and in a spirit of solemn dedication.

However, we have to face the fact that marriages between Christian people, who started off with the best of intentions, do sometimes break down. What are we to say when this happens?

On this point the Church is divided. The Catholic tradition takes the view that the letter of the law must be strictly observed in this matter. When two Christian people find that their marriage relationship means little or nothing to them, they must bear their hardship with fortitude, as a soldier endures hardship in the service of his country. If they feel they cannot go on living together, they must nevertheless accept the fact that, though separated, they are still man and wife. Divorce and re-marriage are out of the question. In this way, it is believed, the sanctity and honour of the institution of Christian marriage are preserved.

Some non-Catholics share this interpretation. But most Protestants accept divorce, though only with deep regret and as a last resort when all efforts to mend the marriage have failed. They consider that the rigid views takes no account of human frailty. People with the best intentions are capable of making serious mistakes in judgement, or of attempting something which they prove unable to carry out. While there is no question that the truly Christian marriage represents a lifetime commitment, there are other marriages which simply cannot fulfil the divine purpose, because they bring no true love or happiness to husband, wife, or children. In such a situation, compassion should be exercised, and divorce and re-marriage permitted.

These two opposing views are not easily reconciled. But both sides will agree that the intention and hope for every Christian marriage is that it will last throughout all the years in which both partners remain alive; not only so, but that it will fill those years with so much joy and gladness, so much mutual affection and mutual devotion, that the idea of going their separate ways will never be seriously entertained by either partner.

What this means is not only to choose each other with great care, but also to work at the tasks of marriage with great diligence. In this respect it is the duty and privilege of Christian couples to set an example of constancy and devotion to each other. It is very easy, when others around us are lax and careless, to neglect our ideals and lower our standards. Yet in such times as these, the witness of good Christian marriage is needed not less, but much more, than it has ever been before. The Christian's standards are high; he accepts them gladly and willingly as part of the way of life which he has voluntarily chosen.

The great error of the past has been that Christian people were not content with binding this high ideal upon themselves, and seeking by the quality of their married life to show forth the Christian way; they tried to impose these standards on others against their will. The day in which it was possible to do that kind of thing is all but over for the Christian Church; and some of us at least are not at all sorry.

Yet we are still in danger of doing something very similar— of passing harsh judgements on, and even rejecting, people whose marriages have failed and who have had to resort to divorce. There is no justification for those of us who are blessed with happy marriages to adopt a 'holier-than-thou' attitude to acquaintances—even fellow-members of our churches—who are less fortunate. A broken marriage is a tragic experience, and those who are going through such an experience deserve not our condemnation, but our compassion.

PRAYER

We thank Thee, O God, for the long years of happiness together which married life promises us. Yet we do not expect that the way will always be easy. If days of hardship should come, help us to meet them in a spirit which may set a good example to others. And enable us always to be loving and understanding toward those less fortunate than ourselves. Amen.

Part 2

THE INTIMACIES OF MARRIAGE

1. *Belonging to One Another*

As Christ loved the church, even so ought husbands also to love their own wives as their own bodies. He that loveth his own wife loveth himself.

EPHESIANS $5^{25, 28}$

Let the husband and wife avoid a curious distinction of mine and thine; for this hath caused all laws, and all the suits, and all the wars in the world.

JEREMY TAYLOR—*The Marriage Ring*

In this holy estate which the contract preceded, and the consummation initiated, there was a marvellous oneness of holy life, a sense of mutual yearning mysteriously satisfied in a peacefulness of mutual possession, an interpretation of the life of each in that of the other, all in fact which is implied in that mighty mystery, which no man will ever comprehend in all the depths of its far reaching sympathies.

OSCAR D. WATKINS—*Holy Matrimony*

Married love is the dynamic unity of human nature, working between two human beings under specially favourable conditions. Such favourable conditions are found nowhere in the order of nature, except between husband and wife, because two persons of different sex, who love each other, are more adapted for union without injury to their individual natures, than persons in any other form of merely human association.

E. MERSCH—*Love, Marriage, and Chastity*

WHEN we speak of the intimacies of marriage, most people naturally think of sex. That is certainly an important part of marital intimacy, and we shall consider it from many different

33

points of view. But before we do so, let us recognize that sexual union can achieve its full purpose only between two people who already feel that they belong to each other in a wider and deeper sense. The kind of casual experience in which a man and woman meet, come together sexually, and part without further interest in each other, is an animal pattern rather than a human one. The sex relationship attains its fullest range of meaning only when it takes place between two people who have a deep knowledge of each other as persons, and are committed to a permanent sharing of life at all its levels.

In no other adult human relationship do people come as close together as in marriage. It is a terrifying closeness, because it means that married people surrender their right to a completely private life of their own. They unveil their bodies and their hearts to each other, accepting each other for what they are. This is costly, and requires courage and trust. Yet unless you can do it, you cannot experience the full meaning of married life. There are many people who, although they are married and sharing the same home, are really living apart. They have been unable to face the intimacies of marriage.

St. Paul talks of married people loving each other as they love their own bodies. This means that, in relation to each other, they have put away shame and false modesty about bodily functions or bodily blemishes. They have accepted each other as they have had to accept themselves—as they are. They have identified themselves with one another, so that each partner naturally strives to ease pain and discomfort in the other as if it were a personal experience. As Edward Carpenter put it, a husband or wife should be a person 'whose body is as dear to one, in every part, as one's own'.

Because of this mutual acceptance, husbands and wives are able to perform many lowly ministries for each other. In sickness their tender familiarity enables the one to care for the other as no other person possibly could. All this, as well as sexual union, is part of the meaning of the intimacy of marriage. Indeed, the wider acceptance of each other physically may prove, for some couples, to be a more difficult and delicate task than the recognition of each other's sexual needs.

We must therefore accept the fact that the intimacies of marriage mean the invasion of our privacy, the tearing down of our pretences. But the sense of belonging to one another brings rich and satisfying compensations. The Greeks had a curious legend that in the beginning men and women were joined together in pairs, that the Gods in a capricious moment divided and separated them, and that in love and marriage they rediscovered one another and were reunited. That is actually what happily married people feel about each other. As their bodies come into contact, in the pressure of hand upon hand, the rapture of a kiss, or the satisfying completeness of the sexual embrace, it is as if the deep ache of their hearts is ended and the open wound caused by their severance from one another healed at last.

PRAYER

O Thou to whom all hearts are open, all desires known; grant us the courage to live together, as husband and wife, in such mutual intimacy that we may heal each other's wounds, meet each other's needs, and enrich each other's lives. Amen.

2. *The Blessing of Sexual Union*

Have ye not read, that he which made them from the beginning made them male and female. And the twain shall become one flesh?

MATTHEW 19[4, 5]

It is important to realize that the (sexual) passion is not just tolerated in marriage, condoned as rather unworthy yet all the same necessary. It leads up to and is present in sacramental marriage, and there finds its complete and gracious expression. Sex intercourse enjoyed rightly and in a human way is an act of the virtue of purity. It is none the colder for that. Purity is not the absence or denial of passion, but is passion justly ordered. In this matter a married couple will help one another. Their bodies are granted, their passions satisfied, not by indulgence, for that defeats its own end, but by a human act full of grace, that does not diminish, but rather increases the ardour, even the passion, of love.

T. G. WAYNE—*Morals and Marriage*

To those who are conscious of spiritual realities it seems more consonant with truth to think of love, not as derived from sex, but as an ultimate value revealed through the workings of sex. Sex is a human happening in time and space. Love is eternal in the heavens: but sex provides the medium through which love's earthly work can be accomplished and such work is creative on all its planes.

E. D. HUTCHINSON—*Creative Sex*

And if in the end husband and wife attain the climax of free and complete union, then their human play has become one with the divine.

HAVELOCK ELLIS—*Little Essays of Love and Virtue*

THE Bible has no hesitation in declaring that the sexual nature of man was deliberately created as part of the divine purpose. The hand of the Creator did not falter or slip at this point. The Hebrews accepted this view of sex wholeheartedly. For them the sexual union of husband and wife was a blessing bestowed by God for man's enjoyment and use.

Unfortunately this has not always been the attitude of the Christian Church. The history of Christendom has been shadowed by a distorted fear of sex. This attitude is not found in the original teaching and intention of Jesus. It has crept in as a result of false doctrines and unhealthy influences. Only in recent years have we been able to see a gradual but welcome change in the generally accepted Christian attitude towards sex.

There are good reasons why devout Christian people should have gained the impression that man's sexual nature was an obstacle to his spiritual progress. In the pagan world, where the Christian message was first preached, sexual excesses of a degrading kind were widely practised. In warning young converts against these dangers, it was easy to give the impression that all sexual urges represented the promptings of the devil. It is as true today as it was then, and as it always will be, that if men and women fall under the tyranny of their sexual impulses their moral and spiritual development will suffer. But the fact that sex can easily be abused does not mean that it is evil or shameful. To adopt that attitude will be a hindrance to us, and not a help. For most people the best way to guard against abusing sex is to put it to its proper use.

It is of the greatest importance that Christian husbands and wives should understand this. Many of us were brought up under the still lingering influence of the old tradition. Somewhere in our deepest thoughts and feelings there may still lurk doubts about the wholesomeness of the sex side of marriage. There may still seem to us to be something just a little unclean or shameful or discreditable about the fact that we have sexual intercourse from time to time with our wives or husbands. It cannot be strongly enough asserted that there is no authoritative Christian truth which gives any support to such feelings or attitudes.

Before we go on to discuss the sexual life in marriage, we should try to get this issue really clear. If you have misgivings about the essential goodness of marital intercourse, you ought to examine them carefully and conscientiously. Don't be distressed if you find yourself in this position. You are in distinguished company. Even Martin Luther said: 'It is not possible to pray upon the marriage bed'. Yet if we believe in progress in the understanding and interpretation of Christian truth, we must be prepared to acknowledge that in this matter Luther had not fully seen the light. By way of contrast, consider these words written by T. G. Wayne in a book about the modern Catholic attitude: 'Since it may be full of grace, there is no obligation to forego intercourse on the night before Holy Communion. If both have been contented in a human manner and excess has been avoided, there is nothing unworthy in the action or its after-effects; the mind is left clear and content and prepared for prayer.'

Christian married couples owe it to each other to reach complete agreement on this important issue. They should talk it over together freely and frankly. So long as there remain any feelings of shame or guilt in their attitude to sexual union, their spiritual as well as their physical relationship will suffer in consequence.

The Creation story tells us that God, after He had made the world and its inhabitants—including man and woman and the sexual nature which defines the difference between them—looked on the finished work and declared that it was 'very good'. Christian husbands and wives, as they come together in the deeply satisfying experience which fulfils their nature and the purposes for which it was ordained, should be able to echo the Creator's joy and satisfaction and reverently to give thanks for the blessing of sexual union.

PRAYER

O Thou whose infinite wisdom has made us male and female, and ordained that in the expression of married love we should become one flesh; enable us to rejoice together in this great gift, and to find in it a source of ever-increasing joy and peace. Amen.

3. *Meeting Each Other's Needs*

Let the husband render unto the wife her due; and likewise also the wife unto the husband. The wife hath not power over her own body, but the husband: and likewise also the husband hath not power over his own body, but the wife. Defraud ye not one another.

1 CORINTHIANS 7^{3–5}

The phase of relations in which conflict first originates is that of sex. This is probably true because it is the earliest relationship demanding an adjustment.

HARRIET R. MOWRER—*Personality Adjustment and Domestic Discord*

I do not mean that a satisfactory marital relationship is the most important thing in life. But I do believe, and with good reason, that it is essential to a happy married life and that to a considerable extent all else revolves round it. I believe that practically every divorce is a result, directly or indirectly, of either definite sexual unhappiness or the absence of positive sexual happiness. It is then that little differences of opinion become incompatibilities. Without the common ground of the mutual and intimate expression of love, the gradual separation of the paths of husband and wife, with or without divorce, is almost inevitable.

FREDERICK LOOMIS—*Consulting Room*

The physical basis of marriage is all-important . . . If it is all awry, the most fortunate constitutions, the most delicate sentiments, the strongest characters, the most generous and well-informed deliberations will hardly succeed in making the marriage a happy one: and it is much if they can prevent it from going to pieces on the rocks.

WILLIAM MCDOUGALL—*Character and the Conduct of Life*

HAVING considered the importance of right *attitudes* to sex, we must go further, and see how attitudes affect *actions*.

When married people regard sex with feelings of fear, guilt, or shame, the whole fellowship of the marriage may be greatly endangered. Such people will try to avoid sexual intimacy, to suppress in themselves and each other all promptings of physical desire. For people endowed with normal impulses, this can only be done at great cost. In a relationship as close as marriage, the vigorous suppression of the natural urge towards physical union can set up strong biological tensions. These will thrust up into all the other areas of the relationship—mental, emotional, spiritual—and create acute strain and irritation.

When this begins to happen, the couple may seek a solution by avoiding all physically stimulating contacts and withdrawing from one another. The healthy intimacy of married life cannot be sustained if the normal and appointed expression of that intimacy is denied. So the couple who cannot be happy in their sex relationship will tend to avoid the affectionate endearments which normally lead up to full union. The warmth and tenderness of their love will wane. Soon small disagreements will seem like major issues between them, and resentment will be stirred up at the slightest difference of opinion. With the loosening of the sexual bond they will begin to drift apart.

Of course, there are great variations between one couple and another, and sexual intimacy does not have the same degree of importance for all. There are times, also, when for good reason husbands and wives must set aside their physical needs. But experience shows again and again that neglect of the sex life in marriage leads to danger and sometimes disaster. To imagine that there is any virtue in such neglect is to deny the divine purpose and to reject the divine gift.

To act like this is also to fail your marriage partner. There was a time when men talked of the 'marriage rights', meaning that wives must be prepared to submit to sexual intercourse whenever their husbands demanded it. Fortunately we have now outgrown such crude and one-sided concepts of marriage. Yet, while we reject the idea of marriage rights, we must not forget that there are marriage duties—not so much duties defined by law, but duties dictated by love. One of these is the duty not to condemn your marriage partner to suffer a state of unrelieved sexual frustration. If you do this, you are asking for sustained love and loyalty while you are withholding the experience of unity in which the love and loyalty of married couples are continually regenerated. This is unfair. St. Paul put it in stronger terms. He said that you are practising a fraud. You are not in fact giving, as part of the marriage contract, what in the eyes of the world you have undertaken to give to your wife or husband.

However, husbands and wives who act in this way do not as a rule do so intentionally. Often there is not awareness of the hurt that is being caused. Christian husbands and wives are sometimes very ignorant about the sexual side of marriage. They may even think that this is an unspiritual or improper subject. That is a serious error. Married couples who call themselves Christians owe it to one another to take their sex relationship seriously; to give themselves to it wholeheartedly, striving to invest it with all the warmth and richness which it should have: for it is the God-given and sacramental expression of their mutual love.

PRAYER

Grant us, O Lord, such kindness and consideration in our married love that we may always be quick to sense each other's needs and ready to meet them. Thus may our mutual affection and devotion never wither, but continually increase. Amen.

4. *When Two Become One*

So they are no more twain, but one flesh.

MATTHEW 19[6]

The sex relationship is as 'unnatural' as street-cars or a Beethoven symphony. It is the product of human patience, intelligence, skill. The sex behaviour of the lower animals and of undeveloped races is more or less casual, largely self-centred. It does not enrich the experience of sexual mates. This mutuality in the sexual relationship is an artistic achievement, and artistic achievements do not just happen.

FREDERICK HARRIS—The World Tomorrow

You know all that should come before?—the happiness of waiting; the loving words he says to me; the tender whispers which I save just for him; the so shaded light; the pretty nightdress which I am so lucky to have though we are all so poor; the kisses—all these we call the preludium, as if we were going to the symphony.

And after—ah, after, when he is even more tender to me, when I finally go to sleep with my head upon his shoulder, and our hearts are singing and our spirits are content—why, then we say it is the postludium, because we have indeed been to so sweet a symphony.

Quoted by FREDERIC LOOMIS in The Consultation Room

When the wave of love is once set in motion, there is then no shastra and no order. Any action on the part of the husband or the wife which creates love or intensifies it on the other side is perfectly in accordance with the rules of the Kama Shastra.—

J. H. VATSYAYANA, in the Kama Sutra, sacred book of India.

THE proper use of sex, according to all reliable Christian teaching, is to be a blessing to married people. This it does in two ways. It has a unitive function, and it has a procreative function.

In the Bible the greatest emphasis is given to the unitive function—both in the account in Genesis of the creation of man and woman, and in what Jesus said about the origin of marriage. No doubt it was considered unnecessary to emphasize the procreative function; partly because it was obvious, and partly because it was believed that it would follow automatically when the unitive function was fulfilled.

The unitive function of sex is to consummate the unity of husband and wife when their marriage begins, and continuously to renew and sustain that unity as they go on through life together. It will achieve this end only if it is a mutually satisfying experience. Where intercourse is clumsily or carelessly or casually performed it may easily defeat its own end, and bring disappointment and disgust instead of gratitude and delight. Where one partner is seeking to take only and not to give, to achieve individual gratification rather than to bestow happiness, the result may be resentment, and not contentment. If sexual union is to be a blessing, therefore, it must be approached with intelligent understanding and loving consideration.

What this means is that husband and wife must together learn the art of mutually satisfying intercourse. This will require time and patience. It is the greatest mistake to imagine that all we have to do is to respond to the blind promptings of impulse and all will be well. We are not animals; and as human beings, we have to learn to control and direct all our physical impulses so that they serve, and do not thwart, the higher ends of human living.

No two married couples are exactly alike, and there will be wide differences in the patterns which suit them best. Each couple must have confidence in working out the arrangement which meets their particular needs. Often people will read books about sexual technique and then become unsettled because their experience does not fit the pattern which is described. There is no absolutely right way in which the sex relationship should be conducted. It is the end which matters, not the means. Whatever brings a couple to a state of mutual happiness, contentment, and peace is right for that couple. The function of sexual union is to create and recreate the sense of unity—the feeling that husband and wife are no longer two, but are made one through the flesh. If they enter into that experience when they come together sexually, all is well.

For most couples the experience is best attained when they can achieve mutual and simultaneous orgasm, reaching the sexual climax together so that for a moment they lose the sense of their individual identity and their spirits seem to flow into one another. It is worth striving to reach that carefully timed mutual ecstasy. But it is not essential to do so. Many couples find it too difficult to achieve, and rather than doom themselves to frequent frustration they are content to help each other in turn to reach the sexual climax. Sometimes the wife, and occasionally the husband also, will be unable to reach the climax at all, or will have no desire to make the effort and risk failure and frustration. Yet the satisfying sense of the closest bodily intimacy can bring to such couples the experience of unity that is desired. So long as they are content, finding the fulfilment of their sexual needs in and through each other, the unitive function will be achieved.

The secret of success lies in complete mutual understanding, a sincere desire in each partner to make the other happy, and plenty of time to make the experience free from all hurry or haste. Far from being a hindrance to the spiritual life, sexual union under those conditions can be, and for Christian couples should be, in every sense an act of worship.

PRAYER

And when we meet breast to breast, O God, may it be upon thine own. Amen.

From the diary of Temple Gairdner, before his marriage

5. *Attaining Sexual Harmony*

Stir not up, nor awaken love, until it please.

SONG OF SONGS 2[7]

If men and women act according to each other's liking, their love for each other will not be lessened even in one hundred years.

VATSYAYANA in the *Kama Sutra*

The direction and proper use of the erotic craving is one of the duties and disciplines of life. Sex is a potentiality that cannot be underrated or trifled with, and still less ignored. There scarcely exists a man or woman who can assert complete immunity from emotional unrest, mental difficulties, ethical dilemmas, or physical signs related to the sex life. The vital urge is always more or less active within us.

WALTER M. GALLICHAN—*The Psychology of Marriage*

I do think people ought to be told how important physical love is— just because of how it can add to the other side of love. But we aren't told that, by the people who specialize in the other side of loving; and the people who specialize in the physical side don't seem to know or care about the other. So the two things are sort of set apart in our minds, instead of being brought together.

ANN BRIDGE—*Four-Part Setting*

THE task of married lovers is not simply to learn the art of sexual union, so that each occasion of their coming together is a mutually satisfying experience. They must also fit their physical love-making into the total pattern of their shared life, in such a way as to make allowance for the varying needs of each and for the circumstances in which they live. To do this well requires consideration and adaptability on both sides.

First, there is the question of frequency. Here again, individual couples must not take text-book standards too seriously. If the average frequency of intercourse among married couples in general is twice a week, it does not follow that you will acquire any particular merit by making your pattern coincide with the average. There are in fact wide variations between one couple and another, and the only standard to be applied is that what suits John and Mary best will be right for them. They must find out by experience how to steer a middle course between frustration on the one hand and excess on the other. Husbands and wives who do not have sexual union often enough become tense and irritable towards their partners. If this state of affairs continues, their affections may wander elsewhere, and they may find themselves vulnerable to temptations which would otherwise not trouble them. If, on the other hand, they have too frequent intercourse, the quality of each act of union may deteriorate until it becomes a monotonous routine. Something between those two extremes is the ideal to be aimed at.

This task of adjustment may be complicated by the fact that the needs of husband and wife do not correspond. This does not mean that they are sexually incompatible; it simply means that they have to work out a compromise together. To some extent all married couples have to do this. In the early months of their life together, for example, the husband as a rule desires intercourse more frequently than the wife. Where there is real love and understanding, these problems of varying need can be met without serious difficulty. The practice of reasonable self-control is essential to successful sex adjustment in marriage. There is no greater mistake than to imagine that the fact of being married gives one partner unlimited sexual access to the other. To act on this assumption is one of the quickest routes to disaster.

It should be understood, therefore, that there may be occasions when either husband or wife may be justified in saying 'No' to the other. But it should be said with warm understanding, so that it is not taken as a rebuff. Many married people are acutely sensitive about making known their sexual desires to each other, and a blunt refusal may hurt them so much that they will be reluctant to make another approach later. Care should be taken, also, not to say 'No' too often. An understanding partner will make a point of responding whenever it is possible to do so, even if only a limited or modified form of sexual union can be offered. True lovers are always glad to give happiness, even on occasions when they cannot personally share it.

The choosing of the right times for intercourse also requires insight and resourcefulness. If the wife is more responsive on certain days than at other times, the husband will accommodate himself to her variations of feeling. They will both try to co-operate in securing the uninterrupted privacy that is necessary for unhurried love-making. Too many couples, as their commitments increase and the pressure of life's many duties bears down upon them, allow their sex life to be crowded into the hours when they are least able to do justice to it. This is folly. They are not only letting each other down, but also depriving themselves of a source of refreshment which should help them to meet the strains of the daily round.

The attainment of sexual harmony is one of the tasks which every married couple must undertake. It depends far less upon biological factors than upon those virtues of kindness, courtesy, and consideration for others which should be cultivated by every Christian.

PRAYER

Grant us, Lord, a sense of proportion, that we may not be so preoccupied with living that we leave no time for loving. Amen.

6. Planned Parenthood

Lo, children are an heritage of the Lord: and the fruit of the womb
is his reward. As arrows in the hand of a mighty man, so are the
children of youth.

PSALM 127³⁻⁴

Young people who wish to have children often delay too long from
economic causes, or from a natural desire not to put a strain on their
first happiness. Yet it is doubtful if to have any instinct too long unfulfilled is not dangerous. Economic reasons and the general unstable
condition of the world are severe handicaps to producing children.
Yet children are good for each other, good for their parents, and good
for the community.

PHYLLIS BOTTOME—And So We Got Married

Scientific contraception, while serving a purpose in assisting married
couples to regulate the spacing of their children, becomes a danger
when misused to enable selfish and irresponsible people to escape the
duties and disciplines of marriage and parenthood.
One of the Ten Principles of the British Marriage Guidance Council

Let us, then, make parenthood the most responsible, the most deliber-
ate, the most self-conscious thing in life, so that there shall be children
born to those who love children, and only to those who love children.
In a generation bred on these principles—a generation consisting only
of babies who were loved before they were born, there would be a
proportion of sympathy, of tender feeling, and of all those great,
abstract, world-creating passions which are evolved from the tender
emotion, such as no age hitherto has seen.

ARTICLE IN 'THE EUGENICS REVIEW'

WE have seen that the sexual union of married people fulfils
two functions—unitive and procreative. From the point of
view of society, the procreative is the more important, because
it is the guarantee that the stream of life shall continue from
generation to generation. But from the point of view of the

couple the unitive end is the more fundamental. Before children come, while they are being brought up, after they have gone, even when there can be no children, sexual intercourse continues to play a vital part in married life. This is fully recognized in the teaching of the Bible. The view that sexual intercourse in marriage is right only when its purpose is to produce children is a false and mischievous distortion of Christian truth.

The Hebrews did not in fact believe that children came simply as a result of the regular sexual intercourse of husband and wife. For a wife to conceive, there must be, in addition, the direct intervention of God, who alone had power to open and close the womb. The coming of a child, therefore, was viewed as a special mark of the divine favour.

Nowadays we can no longer take that simple view. Man himself has in some measure achieved the power of granting or withholding conception which was once attributed solely to God. And with that power comes a new and perplexing responsibility.

There are still married couples who are content to exercise the unitive function of sex and let the procreative function take care of itself. But there are others—especially those who find themselves highly fertile—who are confronted with the need to separate the two functions. More and more of these people—and there are many Christian couples among them— are turning to scientific contraception for the solution of their problem.

When married people, without weighty reasons, avoid parenthood altogether they are failing to fulfil one of the appointed ends of marriage. But the number of couples who refuse to embark upon parenthood merely to suit their own convenience is small. For the great majority, what is desired is to control the procreative function in order to discharge the duties of parenthood in a thorough and responsible way. Such couples want to have time to make ready for the arrival of the first baby; or to space their children in such a way that they can promote their highest well-being; or to limit their family so as to do full justice to each member. They believe in parenthood; but they want it to be planned parenthood.

There is a great diversity of opinion among Christian people today as to whether this is right or wrong. It is important to notice, however, just what the disagreement is about. The principle that a couple may be right in limiting the number of children they bring into the world is not questioned. No Christian body insists that Christian married people must produce the maximum number of children which is physically possible. What is in dispute is the means which may be used by Christian husbands and wives to limit their families when they are satisfied that they are right in doing so. Some believe that the only permissible way is to refrain from intercourse altogether, cutting off the unitive function in order to prevent the procreative. Others consider that they are justified in using the so-called 'safe period' or 'rhythm method', confining intercourse to certain days in the wife's monthly cycle when she is somewhat less likely to conceive. Yet others see nothing wrong in using scientific devices prescribed by competent medical authorities for the control of conception.

As in the case of divorce, Christian people take up opposite and apparently irreconcilable attitudes on this subject. Most of those who belong to the Catholic group hold that it is wrong to use any mechanical or chemical device to prevent conception. Most Protestants, on the other hand, welcome contraception as a means by which they can plan their families and yet continue to enjoy fully the blessings of their sex life.

This is a matter on which Christian married couples must make their own decision. Those who consider contraceptives wrong must be careful to avoid the undue thwarting of the unitive function of marital intercourse. Those who consider contraceptives right must avoid the undue thwarting of the procreative function.

PRAYER

O God, who hast given us the power to create new life in Thine own image; give us also the wisdom to use that power aright. Amen.

7. The Sacrament of Love

Then my lover put his hand through the opening of the door, And my whole heart went out to meet him.

SONG OF SONGS 5[4]

Lovers in their play are moving among the highest human activities, alike of the body and of the soul. They are passing to each other the sacramental chalice of that wine which imparts the deepest joy that men and women can know. They are subtly weaving the invisible cords that bind husband and wife together more truly and more firmly than the priest of any church.

HAVELOCK ELLIS—*Little Essays of Love and Virtue*

Normal sexuality as a common and similarly directed experience, strengthens the feeling of unity and of identity. This condition is described as one of complete harmony, and is extolled as a great happiness ('one heart and one soul') and with reason. It is indeed a true and undeniable experience of divinity, the transcending power of which blots out and consumes everything individual: it is a real communion.

C. G. JUNG—*Contributions to Analytical Psychology*

That I may come near to her, draw me nearer to Thee than to her; that I may know her, make me to know thee more than her; that I may love her with the perfect love of a perfectly whole heart, cause me to love thee more than her and most of all.

That nothing may be between me and her, be thou between us, every moment. That we may be constantly together, draw us into separate loneliness with thyself. And when we meet breast to breast, O God, let it be upon thine own—

From the diary of Temple Gairdner as he prepared for marriage

THE accepted definition of a sacrament is that it is 'the outward and visible sign of an inward and spiritual grace'. In the technical sense of the word, the sexual union of husband and wife is not a sacrament. But it is certainly, when rightly performed, sacramental, in the sense that what happens at the physical level is not all, and not even the most important part, of the experience.

Many of our mistaken ideas about sex come from our observation of animals. The mating of animals may sometimes seem more like a brutal assault than an act of love. Of course there is actually nothing unwholesome about the sexual behaviour of animals, so long as we remember that they *are* animals. But when the sexual behaviour of human beings is merely animal, it is indeed unwholesome; because sex in human experience has far wider and deeper meanings, and our human nature is degraded if we ignore them.

Francis Herries, in Hugh Walpole's novel, speaks of sex in a disillusioned way which many others will echo. 'What do you get? . . . Something. Nothing. And what is there to get? A little hugging and fumbling, sweating and panting, and then satiety.' It is quite true that sexual union can be just that. For many people it *is* just that. For people who approach it in terms of 'What do you get?' and never think of it in any other terms, the end is bound to be disillusionment and satiety.

What is the difference between love and lust? In both the physical mechanisms are exactly the same. What is desired in both cases is the meeting of two bodies. Yet the two experiences are poles apart. What makes the difference? Surely it is the fact that in love the inward and spiritual quality is present, while in lust it is absent. To lust is animal, to love is human.

This means that the more spiritually mature you are, the more sacramental will marital intercourse be for you. If you approach it thinking only of what you are going to *get*, you will get very little. If, however, your chief concern is what you can *give* to enrich the one you love, you will get a great deal for your own enrichment also. If both partners approach it in this spirit, their hearts will soon overflow with love and gratitude.

We often talk about sexual intercourse as 'making love'. Strictly speaking, that is not true. The meeting of two bodies cannot make love. It can only express and enrich a love which is already there. And the quality of the experience will depend upon the quality of the love which it expresses.

Whether they recognize it or not, therefore, married people express in their coming together sexually the whole meaning and quality of their relationship. Their sexual union is consequently a most searching test of what their whole marriage means to them. When their fellowship is warm and strong, they are sexually drawn to each other. When their fellowship is impaired, their sexual interest in each other withers away. 'What is the use of continuing a sex relationship,' as one wife put it, 'when there is nothing left for it to express?'

We have already seen how, when the sex life in marriage is ignored, the resulting frustrations will have a destructive influence upon the harmony of the couple at the other levels of their relationship. This close interaction, however, works both ways. A decline in the fellowship of the marriage will equally disrupt the working of the sexual function, and ultimately destroy it altogether. When two people cease to love one another as persons, their desire to come together sexually usually withers away.

The satisfying physical intimacy of married love can only endure, therefore, if it is more than merely physical. With terrifying ease, physical attraction can turn to revulsion when something happens to estrange the hearts and minds of those whose bodies have sought comfort in each other. Marriage, in fact, is all of a piece. You cannot isolate the physical from the spiritual. They belong together. The one sustains and fortifies the other. The spiritual redeems and ennobles the physical, the physical expresses and communicates the spiritual. Married love cannot endure unless it is sacramental.

PRAYER

O God, who hast revealed the divine love to us in the Word become flesh; enable us, who are joined together in the fellowship of marriage, to establish our human love in a true harmony of body, mind, and spirit. Amen.

Part 3

THE FELLOWSHIP OF MARRIAGE

1. *Meant for Each Other*

Heirs together of the grace of life.

1 PETER 3⁷

Day after day passes and I only get more and more convinced about it: everything else has been laid aside, occupation, sleep and food. And I have sought His face and to know His will, and He has led me straight forward and gives me encouragement and emboldens me to ask for you.

C. T. STUDD, writing to his future wife

She understood him; he felt she did; understood him as, if a man be understood by one woman in the world, he—and she too—is strong, safe and happy. They grasped hands once more, and gazed unhesitatingly into each other's eyes. All human passion for the time being set aside, these two recognized each in the other one aim, one purpose, one faith; something higher than love, something better than happiness.

MRS. CRAIK—*John Halifax, Gentleman*

My true-love hath my heart, and I have his,
By just exchange one for another given;
I hold his dear, and mine he cannot miss,
There never was a better bargain driven.
My true-love hath my heart, and I have his.

SIR PHILIP SIDNEY

THE friends of a well-matched couple often say: 'Those two were made for each other.' That is always a dangerous idea. It suggests that their personalities will fit perfectly, that they will have no mutual adjustments to make, that the full fellowship of marriage will come to them without effort. Such a thing never happens in real life. It is just as well: for often we do not prize highly what costs us nothing.

From a scientific point of view, a man or woman could achieve a successful marriage with any one of a number of eligible persons of the opposite sex. The idea of the 'soul-mate', the 'Mr. Right' for whose appearance on the horizon the sighing maiden wistfully waits, is dismissed as sentimental nonsense. John happens to marry Jane; but he might have been equally happy if he had married Jean or June. Dr. Johnson, in answer to a question from Boswell, gave it as his opinion that marriages on the whole would be just as successful if the partners were chosen for each other by an official of the State, as they are when the man and woman choose each other.

There is obviously a good deal of truth in all this. But for Christian people the scientific view by itself is not enough. If John believes in divine guidance, he will have sought earnestly, in a matter so important as marriage, to make the right choice. It may be true that he could have been happy if he had married Jean or June. It may even be true that with Jean or June he might have created a truly Christian home. Yet he believes that in marrying Jane he did what God most wanted for both of them. Sharing his faith, Jane also believes that, although either Jim or Joe would have made her a good husband, the fact that John was the one she married was providential, and not just accidental.

The belief that they were meant for each other is fundamental to the way in which many Christian husbands and wives consider their marriage. Being meant for each other is not the same as being made for each other. It does not mean that there will not be difficult adjustments to make, hard roads to travel. But it does mean that their fellowship rests on a firm foundation of faith in each other which will greatly fortify them both. When life with Jane is difficult, John will have an answer to his doubts as to whether after all he might not have fared better with someone else; and he will not be so readily assailed by the temptation to give up and end it all. A strong sense of common purpose, a conviction amid all other uncertainties that their destinies are inter-twined, can provide the Christian married couple with an indomitable will to toil together for the fulfilment of the dreams they dreamed together when they took their vows at the altar. They can rest content in the assurance that because their choice of each other was not theirs alone, their life together is enriched by the divine blessing.

PRAYER

O God, enable us amid the perplexities of this life to hold fast to our faith in an unfolding purpose; and may we ever strive, in our fellowship with each other, to bring all our plans and endeavours within the circle of Thy will. Amen.

2. The Shared Life

Ye husbands, dwell with your wives according to knowledge . . . that your prayers be not hindered. Finally, be ye of one mind.

1 PETER 3⁷⁻⁸

The reasons because of which man and woman ought to be joined in marriage, are to be explained. The first is precisely this companionship sought by the natural instinct of different sex and brought about in the hope of mutual aid, so that each may help the other to bear more easily the troubles of life and to support the weakness of old age.

CATECHISM OF THE COUNCIL OF TRENT

A new and higher form of existence is attained by means of marriage. Each surrenders himself freely to the other in love, to be the means of amplifying and completing the personality of the other, while he also surrenders himself no less freely to receive the same service that he renders. And since this takes place on both sides, the higher life that results is shared by both in common.

I. A. DORNER—*Christian Ethics*

Marriage is the greatest earthly happiness, when founded on complete sympathy.

BENJAMIN DISRAELI, in a letter to Gladstone

DR. HENRY WILSON, when Bishop of Chelmsford, described marriage as being, first and foremost, a 'sanctified friendship'. Even if this quality in the marriage relationship may not be accorded the pre-eminence over all other, it must certainly be given the importance which it deserves. We have already seen that it ranks as one of the three great purposes for which marriage was ordained.

The fear of being alone is the most haunting dread which can assail us. With loved ones near and around us, we can endure and survive great hardships. The child who can resign himself to sit in the dentist's chair so long as he may continue to grasp his mother's hand is illustrating a universal truth about human nature. While there is a warm and reassuring hand to support us, life still has meaning and hope. What we really dread most about death is not the pain or the darkness, but the fact that it is the one journey which we must take without human companionship.

The fellowship of married lovers is not all passion and ecstasy. It is mostly made up of the daily round and the common task. In marriage or out of it, the attempt to escape from the routine of the ordinary experiences is cowardly and futile. Our only hope, if we are to make the task of living satisfying in any lasting way, is to invest the ordinary experiences with a quality which makes them a source of happiness to us. By far the best way of doing this, for most of us, is to share them with another in a bond of mutual sympathy and service. A new discovery, a welcome surprise, a fresh awareness of beauty or truth or goodness—experiences such as these give us twice as much delight when there is someone to whom we can say 'Come and enjoy this with me'. Joys are doubled and sorrows are halved when they can be shared with a close and dear companion. Those who have been widowed often tell us that their moments of deepest pain are those in which they yearn in vain for the reassuring touch of a vanished hand, or are startled to hear again in imagination the echo of a voice that is still.

The deeply satisfying fellowship of marriage does not, however, come to us freely. It has to be cultivated. Above all else, it is the product of a mutual trust which has grown out of the frank and courageous sharing of thoughts and feelings. In the old fairy-tales, when the prince had slain the dragon, routed all his foes, and set the fair maiden free, the customary procedure was that the two sat down together and 'he told her all his heart'. This phrase, in its simple beauty, represents the urge which all lovers feel to open up the casket of their inmost thoughts to one another. It is by no means true that all married people, or even most of them, practise this unreserved mutual openness of heart towards one another. Yet it is likely that, with the rare exception of matters which cannot be confided for some very good reason, the degree to which husbands and wives share their thoughts and feelings represents the degree of depth and quality which they are able to achieve in their mutual fellowship.

How reassuring it is, in a world where we are so often driven to hedge ourselves about with defences and pretences, to be known fully and completely by one other person and still loved, despite all our hidden shames and guilty fears! Whatever the world says about you or does to you, you can continue to believe in yourself while the one person who knows you best believes in you still.

O Thou who, perceiving that it was not good for man to be alone, didst give to him in marriage a help meet for his needs, grant that we be not blind to the resources of comfort and companionship which we have in one another. Amen.

3. *The Partnership of Equals*

There is neither male nor female: for ye are all one in Christ Jesus. And if ye be Christ's, then are ye of Abraham's seed, and heirs according to the promise.

GALATIANS 3[28-29]

We are at last in sight of a time when the full and equal partnership of men and women which Christ proclaimed, and His church has been unable to accept, might be achieved. . . . There is in all the complexity of our times no other issue so urgent, so far-reaching, so critical as this.

CHARLES E. RAVEN in E. D. Hutchinson's *Creative Sex*

Our fathers had a saying about marriage, that if two people ride on a horse, one of the two must ride behind. Today marriage is more like two people riding abreast on the same horse, doing a rather difficult balancing feat and each holding one rein. It's more companionable than the old way, but it's more complicated, and must at times be rather confusing to the horse.

LORD BEVERIDGE in a radio talk

Love one another, but make not a bond of love:
Let it be rather a moving sea between the shores of your souls.
Fill each other's cup, but drink not from one cup.
Give one another of your bread but eat not from the same loaf.
Sing and dance together and be joyous, but let each of you be alone,
Even as the strings of a lute are alone though they quiver with the
    same music. . . .

And stand together yet not too near together:
For the pillars of the temple stand apart,
And the oak tree and the cypress grow not in each other's shadow.

KAHLIL GIBRAN—The Prophet

A TRUE fellowship in marriage is only possible where husband and wife respect each other as individuals and treat each other as equals. The peril in any partnership is that one of the partners should dominate or exploit the other. Married people should be continually alert to this danger.

It has often been claimed that the coming of Christianity brought emancipation to womanhood. In many ways this is true. The teaching of Christ that all men and women are alike the children of God, and therefore of equal value in His sight, had clear and revolutionary implications. It has taken a long time, however, for these implications to be fully carried out in practice. Even St. Paul, though he asserts the principle of the equality of the sexes, gives the impression in some of his writings that the wife is the inferior partner in the marriage relationship. This idea has persisted stubbornly in Christian history. The wife has often been treated as if she were subject to her husband as a child is subject to its parents. It is only in recent years that the principle of marriage as a partnership of equals has come into its own.

It is easy to understand why the full acceptance of this Christian principle has come so slowly. A relationship between a tyrant and a slave is less complicated than a partnership of equals; just as a dictatorship makes less demand upon intelligence and resourcefulness than a democracy. The price which has to be paid for a truly democratic marriage is that each partner must always be ready, before reaching a decision, to take fully into account the opinions and wishes of the other. Apart from the time it takes, this requires a high degree of maturity in both. They must be skilful in team work, good at co-operating with others, resilient enough to practise the give and take of a relationship in which the roles of each may have to change frequently. The kind of marriage which we believe in today is undoubtedly harder to work than the fixed pattern of the past, where the domination of the husband and the submission of the wife were taken for granted. But the new pattern is undoubtedly more just, more democratic, and more Christian.

With the concept of equality goes the need for married people to respect each other as individuals. We have emphasized the closeness and intimacy of marriage. Yet this closeness does not give husband and wife the right to make unreasonable demands, or to invade each other's privacy. There is all the difference in the world between the opening of a flower in the sunshine and the tearing apart of its petals with forced, intruding fingers. So all that is given to each other in the intimacy of marriage must be given freely and spontaneously, never surrendered under duress. There are times when the most happily married people desire to be alone. There is a sturdy independence and individuality in all of us which must be respected even by those whom we love the most. The partnership of equals reaches its highest and most enduring quality when husband and wife are able to co-operate smoothly without ever having to make demands of each other.

PRAYER

Teach us, O Lord, to honour and respect each other, knowing that we are both equally precious in Thy sight, both equally called to share the duties and the joys of marriage. In our unity may there always be room for diversity; in our companionship for solitude; in our fellowship for freedom. Amen.

4. *Masculine and Feminine*

In the day that God created man, in the likeness of God made he him; male and female created he them, and blessed them.

GENESIS 5^{1, 2}

The man is restless while he misses his rib that was taken out of his side; and the woman is restless till she gets under the man's arm, from whence she was taken.

RABBINIC SAYING

The ways of working as well as the consciousness of pleasure in men and women are different. The difference in the way of working, by which men are the actors, and the women are the persons acted upon, is owing to the nature of the male and the female. For a man thinks 'This woman is united with me' and a woman thinks 'I am united with this man'.

VATSYAYANA in the *Kama Sutra*

The sexual difference is in its way the greatest possible difference that can exist, and the union consequently forms a unique relationship. No man, however perfect, feels, knows, or wills precisely in the same way as a typical woman. When these thus diverse become one in love, then there is a unity in diversity. We may even explicitly say that a new operative power becomes the possession of the married persons, for there is in reality a new experience not actually found in the consciousness of any human being without this union of greatest contrasts. It really involves seeing with other eyes—which are still their own—hearing, feeling, judging, willing, acting, helping: and this not by the sacrifice of the personal nature of each, but by its enrichment.

THEODORE VON HAERING—*Ethics of the Christian Life*

WHEN we speak of marriage partners as equals, we speak only half of the truth. As persons who have entered into a partnership, husband and wife should divide the duties and share the privileges. Marriage, however, is not one relationship, but two. It is a relationship between partners; and it is a relationship between lovers. To succeed in marriage it is necessary to succeed in both relationships. To be good partners is not enough. To be good lovers is not enough. It is necessary to be both good partners and good lovers.

In the relationship between two lovers, the idea of equality is foreign and irrelevant. The last thing lovers want is to be equal and alike. What gives them joy in each other is precisely the difference between them, the fact that each is able to contribute what the other lacks. They do not, as lovers, think of themselves as individuals asserting their rights over against each other. They think of themselves as merged in a stimulating and satisfying unity in which they complete and fulfil each other. They are not equal, but reciprocal; not alike, but complementary.

So much emphasis has been placed, in recent years, on the idea of the equality of men and women that the difference between their masculine and feminine natures is often underestimated. Men and women, as persons in society, work together and play together as never before. Because of their continual cultural, social, and vocational contacts they come to feel that they have a very good understanding of one another. When they go into marriage, however, they are faced with a new kind of man–woman relationship in which each is playing a very different role. Often they are startled and bewildered to discover how little real understanding they have of one another. Sometimes they refuse to admit the reality of the difference between them. The man treats his wife as he would another man, and is disconcerted when she fails to respond. The woman expects her husband to understand her, and is annoyed and hurt by his obtuseness and lack of sensitivity. The result can be the worst kind of deadlock, in which each disillusioned partner blames the other in bitternes of spirit. The number of marriages which fail for this reason must be legion.

It is tragic when husband and wife thus lose communication with each other. It means that the very differences which should have united them have in fact divided them. The man was made for the woman and the woman for the man; and when a couple turn this natural attraction into repulsion they are punishing themselves as much as each other. They are quarrelling about the very thing which to the happily married couple is the chief source of their delight.

Nothing brings a greater reward to married people than the determined effort to understand their masculine and feminine differences and the needs which arise out of those differences. When the husband can be to his wife all that she expects a man to be, and when the wife can respond to her husband in the way he desires a woman to respond, both are abundantly fulfilling one another. Such a couple will be bound to one another by a mutual dependence which fills their hearts with affection and gratitude.

PRAYER

We rejoice in the wisdom which made us, man and woman, not alike but each the counterpart of the other. O Thou who hast made us thus for each other, give us the understanding, the patience, and the skill to fulfil Thy purpose, and in the fellowship of our marriage to learn the art of lasting love. Amen.

5. *The Continuous Task of Mutual Adjustment*

Let the husband render unto the wife due benevolence: and likewise also the wife unto the husband.

1 CORINTHIANS 7[3]

> The kindest and the happiest pair,
> Will find occasion to forbear,
> And something every day they live
> To pity and perhaps forgive.
>
> WILLIAM COWPER

A successful marriage is an edifice that must be rebuilt every day. Nothing in our daily life will last if neglected; houses, stuffs, friendships, pleasures. Roofs fall in, love comes to an end. A tile needs refastening, a joint must be repaired, a misunderstanding cleared up. Otherwise bitterness is created; feelings deep down in the soul become centres of infection, and one day, during a quarrel, the abscess breaks, and each is horrified by the picture of himself or herself discovered in the other's mind.

ANDRÉ MAUROIS—*The Art of Living*

In the case of husband and wife whose individualities in their natural state are not at first very favourable to their union, the only thing required is, that they should cleanse the pure metal from the dross. And thus marriage will be for each, as it ought to be, a strengthening and purifying of their personal characters. Neither of them is without faults; but if they are Christians, the faults of the one will bring forth and exercise just the opposite virtues in the other, and by this means they will become more and more able to assist each other in overcoming these faults, and to make their union and happiness more complete.

I. A. DORNER—*Christian Ethics*

No more mischievous fallacy has ever been propagated than the notion that marriage requires no creative effort on the part of those who enter it. Yet it is a fallacy which has been long and stubbornly held. In the past, the chief basis for marriage was that it provided for a mutual exchange of services between a man and a woman. So long as this utilitarian end was achieved, the quality of the fellowship between the partners was not considered to be a matter of great importance. The idea that there was an art in the actual living together of husband and wife, apart from the practical purposes for which they lived together, would never have occurred to many of our forefathers.

Today we have swung to the opposite extreme. The utilitarian view of marriage has given way to the romantic view. Now the practical purposes are considered secondary, and the all-important end is the enjoyment of the relationship. Yet still the real issue is evaded. The happiness of marriage is attributed solely to the emotional state of being 'in love', which is in reality no more than the launching platform which gives it a good start. When this initial emotional impetus spends itself, thousands of modern marriages come to a stop because they have nothing to impel them further upon their way.

The truth is that the rewards of successful marriage, like most rewards, come as the result of hard work. In this, marriage is like most other human experiences; why should we expect it to be otherwise? Marriage is in truth a creative task which requires the sincere and sustained effort of people who are sufficiently informed to know what they are doing and sufficiently mature to be able to do it.

The creative task which is involved in marriage is a continuous process of mutual adjustment. When two people marry, they bring to the relationship the accumulated attitudes and habits which they have formed as a result of years of separate living. It is absurd, surely, to imagine that in their tastes, their views, even their values, they will be in complete agreement. Even if they were, it would be unreasonable to expect that they would always want to do the same thing in the same way at the same time.

It is clear, therefore, that the element of conflict is inherent in the marriage relationship. To pretend otherwise is to evade reality. It is far better to admit this fact, and to go on to recognize that some of the best rewards of marriage come to us as a direct result of facing our conflicts and resolving them. The clash of conflicting wills is not, therefore, a disaster. It is a healthy evidence that an area requiring mutual adaptation has been laid bare in the fellowship of the marriage. The proper response to this discovery is not to despair, but to start work. By intelligent effort the apparent breach can not only be healed: the area of weakness can be turned into an area of strength; as a broken bone, after healing, is often strongest at the point where the break occurred. And the task of making the adjustment can develop in both partners new qualities of character which will make them more understanding and more adaptable.

In the early years of marriage a good deal of this mutual adaptation must take place. The stronger and better equipped the personalities, the greater will be the magnitude of the task. Apart from these major adjustments of the first years, continual resourcefulness is necessary to keep the fellowship of the marriage in good repair. The better the work of building was done in the first place, the less will it be affected later by wear and tear. But to some extent at least the maintenance of a marriage at its best will require constant vigilance. Only upon those husbands and wives who are ready for this are the full rewards of married happiness bestowed.

PRAYER

Save us, O Lord, from the folly of expecting the rewards of marriage without labour; and from the carelessness which, knowing what is necessary, neglects to do it. As we prize our mutual love and fellowship, make us zealous in guarding them from all danger and decay. Amen.

6. Times of Testing

And the rain descended, and the floods came, and the winds blew, and beat upon that house; and it fell not: for it was founded upon the rock.

MATTHEW 7[25]

I, N, take thee N, to have and to hold from this day forward, for better, for worse; for richer, for poorer; in sickness and in health.

THE MARRIAGE SERVICE

All loves and friendships need a certain three days' burial before we can be sure of their truth and their immortality. Mine had likewise its entombment, bitter as brief. Many cruel hours sat I in the darkness, weeping at the door of its sepulchre, thinking I should never see it again; but, in the dawn of the morning, it arose, and I met it in the desolate garden, different, yet the very same. And after that, it walked with me continually, secure and imperishable.

MRS. CRAIK—John Halifax, Gentleman

My wife grew angry; and so, her voice come to her, grew quite out of order, and I to say little, but to bed, and my wife said little also, but could not sleep. After her much crying and reproaching me with inconstancy, I did give her no provocation, but did promise all fair usage to her and love, and foreswore any but that I did with her, till at last she seemed to be at ease again, and so toward morning a little sleep.

SAMUEL PEPYS—Diary

Seldom, or perhaps never, does a marriage develop into an individual relationship smoothly and without crisis; there is no coming to consciousness without pain.

C. G. JUNG—Analytical Psychology

THE process of mutual adjustment in marriage may sometimes break down for a time, producing deadlock: or it may involve the couple in a situation of such intensity that it mounts to a crisis. The Christian knows better than most how frail is human nature, how subject to temptation. To nearly all marriages there come times of testing.

At these times the fellowship of the marriage is in peril. Anger may break through uncontrolled, and words be spoken which are afterwards bitterly regretted. Furtiveness and deceit may be practised in an unworthy attempt to conceal inconstancy. Hearts may be hardened and spirits estranged in a vindictive silence. Husband and wife thus fall out of tune with one another, their harmony shattered and jarring discord in its place. In this atmosphere love can easily turn to hate, trust to suspicion, tenderness to cold indifference.

To weather such storms the married couple need a quality in their love which can transcend self-interest. Desire is a part of love, and not a discreditable part. Friendship, a natural liking for each other, is a part of love also. But when the times of testing come something more is needed. Love must be able to endure for a season even when desire is dead and friendship violated. To do so it must have something of that disinterested concern for the beloved, that sustained solicitude, of which St. Paul has spoken in immortal words. Loving which is no more than liking is without inner resources, and therefore has no power of endurance. A few days in the wilderness and it perishes and withers away.

Whence comes this strength which gives to love its enduring quality? It is not of the mind, nor of the emotions; but of the spirit. The mind records the facts, and reasons. 'Because she has done this', says the outraged husband, 'I am under no further obligation to be kind and considerate towards her'. The emotions react. 'I am hurt and humiliated', says the indignant wife, 'I hate and despise him for treating me like this'. But the spirit whispers: 'There is more to be said. Remember this is the one you have loved tenderly, to whom you pledged your loyalty even for such a time as this. Perhaps there was greater provocation than you know. Remember that you also are weak, that you also have failed and fallen. Be patient. Be generous. Be compassionate.'

The truth is that the whole fellowship of marriage is ultimately based on forgiveness. Two people unable to forgive could not endure to live together as a married couple. That is why courts of law are so clumsy and so helpless in dealing with marriage problems. The law is concerned with offence and retribution, with the neatly balanced justice which makes the punishment fit the crime. In grave matters this principle may be necessary to keep the peace. But so long as marriage remains in any sense a relationship, it must be conducted upon an entirely different principle—the principle of repentance and forgiveness.

Sometimes in marriage it is very hard to forgive. Sometimes full forgiveness must be conditional on a sustained demonstration of genuine repentance. But the readiness to forgive is of the essence of love which can pass through the times of testing and emerge victorious.

PRAYER

O God, before whom none of us dare appear except we know ourselves to be forgiven; teach us, when hopes are deflated and trust betrayed, to bear with each other and be merciful for love's sake. Amen.

7. The Spiritual Pilgrimage

If we love one another, God abideth in us, and his love is perfected in us.

1 JOHN 4[12]

Marriage is worthy to take rank in that subtle and wonderful system of appointed means by which the life of man on earth becomes his school for heaven.

JOHN KEBLE OF OXFORD

The glory of the holy state of matrimony will come into its own, and be regarded no longer as a drag and hindrance to a man's or a woman's spiritual development, but as a sweetening and uplifting power.

SIR FRANCIS YOUNGHUSBAND—*Modern Mystics*

Together they have travelled the road of life, and remembrance now holds them close, remembrance of many hours of ineffable felicity, of a sense of union as near to bliss as mortal hearts can realize, of high aspirations pursued in common, of sorrows shared—sacramental sorrows. And now, nearing the end, hand in hand they look forth upon the wide universe, and the love which they found in themselves and still find there to the last, becomes to them the pledge of a vaster love that moves beyond the stars and the suns.

FELIX ADLER

WHEN Jeremy Taylor said that marriage is 'the nursery of heaven', he threw down a challenge to an attitude which has been all too prevalent in Christian history. Preoccupied with the merits of celibacy, the Church has often failed to recognize that to devout Christian men and women marriage equally can be a spiritual vocation. In the life and activity of the home, as well as in the shuttered seclusion of the monastic cell, men and women can grow in spiritual stature. Each must be free to choose his own way; but it must no longer be said that one way is superior to the other.

The false emphasis on withdrawal from the world, the dark shadow cast upon sexual love, the preoccupation with the utilitarian ends which marriage serves rather than with the value of the relationship itself—these and other influences have diverted attention from the realization that marriage provides unique opportunities to cultivate the Christian graces. It may be that one of the Church's greatest opportunities at the present time is to portray Christian marriage as the setting out of a man and woman, hand in hand, upon a spiritual pilgrimage.

What better way is there to discover the unique qualities of Christian love than in a close relationship where opportunities to practise kindness and unselfishness are never lacking? How much easier it is to sustain a spiritual discipline when two who live together are united in their resolve! How effectively can husband and wife, in their intimately shared life, confess their faults to each other and help and encourage each other to overcome them! If two set out to climb the ladder to heaven together, may they not make better progress than if each climbed alone?

It has often been observed that a marriage has greater security and stability when the partners share a common loyalty outside their relationship which takes precedence even over their loyalty to one another. Temple Gairdner understood this well when he prayed 'That I may love her with the perfect love of a perfectly whole heart, cause me to love Thee more than her and most of all'. It is the recognition of a devotion accepted by each which ranks higher than their devotion to one another that makes a religious marriage essentially different from a marriage based on mutual convenience. Marriage can only be truly a vocation when it is seen as part of a greater vocation still.

This needs to be better understood, and more frequently proclaimed, if many Christian couples are to be saved from a drab mediocrity and encouraged to climb towards the higher reaches of attainment to which their fellowship beckons them. The Church may help and encourage them in this; yet it has no right to impose upon them stereotyped patterns for their spiritual life together. The sense of vocation must come from within, and they must be free to pursue it in the way which together they agree upon.

If there is a special quality about Christian marriage, this fact will not be impressed upon the world by ecclesiastical pronouncements, still less by arrogant denunciations of every other kind of relationship between man and woman. It will declare itself each time a married couple, through sustained mutual faith and unobtrusive witness, show by their example how human love is enriched when it is irradiated with the divine.

PRAYER

May we not rest content, O Lord, with a marriage which is mediocre. Quicken us to all the vast and limitless possibilities of increase in faith and hope and love which open out before us. Separately and together, may we grow continually in grace with the passing years. Amen.

Part 4

THE WIDER IMPLICATIONS OF MARRIAGE

1. *Getting On with In-Laws*

Therefore shall a man leave his father and his mother, and shall cleave unto his wife.

GENESIS 2²⁴

The family of the bride has now to surrender a loved and loving member. They have to give her up to another, to be wholly his, and to take his name. This may well be, and often is, a great sacrifice.

JOHN HOW—The Venture of Christian Marriage

Everyone concerned needs to remember that adjustments have to be made all around, and adjustments take time. Father and mother have to adjust to daughter-in-law exactly as she has to adjust to them. And the process is probably more difficult for them than for her because they are older. Parents cannot quickly alter affection to include someone new, particularly someone with different values. They have bestowed effort and hope and money as well as love in bringing up their child. They cannot change their relationship to him at once.

F. ALEXANDER MAGOUN—Love and Marriage

The mutual assimilation and adjustment of in-laws is not always easy. Anything that can serve to further the process is worth trying. What hinders the process is worth avoiding.

HENRY A. BOWMAN—Marriage for Moderns

MANY unkind words have been spoken about in-laws. The subject has become a standing joke. Often, when we laugh too much about some aspect of our human life, it is because we are secretly aware that it confronts us with a tragedy which defeats us. Our laughter is the way in which we try to discharge our heightened emotional tension.

Let us face the truth. This 'leaving and cleaving' is one of the poignant yet inevitable human experiences. Between parent and child, as the child grows, deep bonds of mutual attachment are forged. Superficially, these are broken as the child matures. But they are not broken at deeper levels. All parents, however bad, invest something of themselves in their children. From this investment they expect, in return, devotion and affection. Often they expect much more.

The marriage of a son or daughter involves, for the parent, an act of surrender. It means taking second place instead of first place, standing down and being supplanted by another. However 'sensible' parents are about this, however fully they approve the choice and desire the happiness and well-being of their child, it is an experience which hurts. There must be few mothers who have not wept secretly on the wedding day of a son or daughter, few fathers whose pride has not been strangely mingled with sadness. The French say that to part is always to die a little. There is a faint shadow of the ominous at every wedding feast.

All this is true under the best conditions. The tension is much greater when complications arise. A parent clinging possessively to son or daughter, or disapproving of the choice which has been made, will witness the marriage with an inward sense of doom. Assailed by the dull ache of frustration which follows, nothing is easier than to release piled-up tension in the form of hostility against the new husband or wife. In such a state of mind, the slightest sign of inadequacy becomes an occasion for furtive persecution or open criticism. Retaliation or resentment only fans the flame and intensifies the parent's feeling of indignation, sometimes to the point of savage vindictiveness.

It is best to be honest and to recognize these possibilities. For all concerned, it is kindest that a complete break be made when the marriage takes place. For a young couple to spend the early days of marriage, the days of critical adjustment, with in-laws is to tempt Providence. Almost any arrangement is to be preferred.

Frank acceptance of the facts on both sides, and resolute goodwill, can surmount this natural crisis experience. By some this is done so well that there is no sense of crisis at all. In other cases time and patience and understanding will bring final harmony between in-laws. The achievement of this harmony is so important that it is worth every effort which can be made. Failure here will have its inevitable distressing overtones within the marriage relationship. There can be no complete contentment for any of us while the two closest relationships in our lives are at variance with each other.

When it is successfully achieved, the grafting together of two families is great gain for all concerned. In-law relationships can become as strong and deep as the bonds of natural kinship. Surely Christian people will make this, and nothing less, their constant aim.

PRAYER

O Thou who hast ordained alike the devotion between parent and child, between husband and wife; grant that we may give our affection not only to those whom it is natural for us to love, but to those also who love them and are loved by them; so that our love and theirs, through the widening of its boundaries, may be multiplied. Amen.

2. Friends and Neighbours

And when he cometh home, he calleth together his friends and his neighbours, saying unto them, Rejoice with me.

LUKE 15⁶

Your behaviour to your husband's particular friends will have the most important effects on your mutual happiness. If you do not accept his sentiments with regard to these, your union must be very incomplete, and a thousand disagreeable circumstances will continually arise from it.

MRS. CHAPONE, in a letter to a bride

Never a week passed without a visit from Mary Wood, my friend in every phase of life. 'How I wish you would be married too', I often said to her. She dropped in at any hour, and shared in any meal. Such visits were always heartily enjoyed.

M. V. HUGHES—*A London Family*

My wife rose by five o'clock in the morning, and went to market and bought fowls and many other things for dinner with which I was highly pleased. My dinner was noble and enough. I had my house mighty clean and neat; my room below with a good fire in it; my dining room above, and my chamber being made a withdrawing-chamber. At night to supper, and sent my guests away about ten o'clock, both them and myself highly pleased with our management of this day; and indeed their company was very fine.

SAMUEL PEPYS—*Diary*

WHEN two people first fall in love, they are intensely preoccupied with one another. They discern all others as vague shadows moving outside the focus of their vision. To be left alone together is their supreme delight.

This desire for withdrawal and seclusion marks the early period of married life. It is recognized and provided for in the institution of the honeymoon. But as the married couple settle down together, they find that their dream of continuing isolation cannot be fulfilled. Their old friends wish to visit them in their new home. They must make new friends in the neighbourhood where they have chosen to live. Invitations are received by them, and other invitations are expected from them. They become aware that to have a home is to incur social obligations.

Not only must both accept a new and closer relationship to the other's family, but also to the other's circle of friends.

During the courtship period friends on both sides obligingly withdraw. But once they are married, it is assumed that old associations will be renewed.

This presents the couple with a somewhat delicate task. All the previous associations cannot in fact be renewed, and it is foolish to think otherwise. John must give up some of his bachelor interests, if only to make time to cultivate with Jane some of the activities which she feels to be important. She must do likewise. There is therefore at this stage a certain inevitable reshuffling of social links in the lives of both of them. Skilfully handled, this can bring them closer to each other, while it widens the horizons of each. Normally it results in each keeping some old friends who are now admitted to the friendship of the other; while at the same time new friends are made who are equally the friends of both of them.

As married life goes on, the couple will tend to make their new friendships together and share them. Yet to insist on this in every case is not reasonable. John may for good reasons want to cultivate someone for whom Jane does not care, and Jane may desire to take part in some activity, important in her eyes, in which John cannot or will not participate. Within reason and by mutual consent, such associations are accepted by most married couples without jealousy or resentment, as part of the give and take of their relationship. It is seldom that two people are completely alike in their individual interests and social habits, and the making of mutual concessions here is a part of every marriage adjustment.

It goes without saying that Christian couples ought to be good neighbours. Families, however perfect, are never complete in themselves. To be fully healthy they need fellowship with other families who share their fundamental standards and values. They even need the stimulus of occasional and limited contact with families of different outlook, if only that they may learn to exercise the virtue of tolerance. In their associations with others they should strive to be, in John Wesley's phrase, 'the friends of all and the enemies of none'. A Christian home should be, in fact, a centre of contagious friendliness, with open doors toward all human need.

May we not forget, O Lord, that we have been called to let our light shine before men. In our life together, may we accept readily the duties as well as the privileges of friendship, seeking to share freely with others the blessings which we have received. Amen.

3. Sharing in the World's Work

And the Lord God said unto Adam, In the sweat of thy face shalt thou eat bread. Therefore the Lord God sent him forth from the garden of Eden, to till the ground from whence he was taken.

GENESIS 3[19, 23]

The connection of marriage with the most important necessities of society gives us to understand that it is not, as most people believe, a private concern. Among the most important requirements for the conclusion of a marriage are therefore a vocation and a livelihood in which both can participate and which insures the support of the family. The vocation, too, is a demand of society, co-operation in production. Likewise, the work of the housewife, at present mistakenly held to be inferior, can create real values, if through good management or artistic enhancement she can increase the man's capacity for labour.

ALFRED ADLER—*Marriage as a Task*

The eager espousal by women of opportunities for labour in the various fields which have been occupied by men is bringing them into relation with collective life. It is giving them a clearer understanding of men and of their lives through their contact with an aspect of man's personality that is never seen under domestic and social conditions. It is this broader field beckoning women away from the narrow personal confines of family life which is giving them the opportunity for growth as individuals, and which is bringing a new attitude to the marriage relation.

BEATRICE M. HINKLE—*Marriage in the New World*

We all occasionally conjure up a dream of leisured ease, of a life of idleness which we would like to enjoy. Few of us ever get the chance, apart from holidays, which are over all too soon, to experience for ourselves what life is like without work. Perhaps it is just as well; for in the main, those few persons who have been able to eat the bread of idleness seem not to have thrived on it. After a time, inactivity and freedom from responsibility seem to have a debilitating effect upon the human constitution. The promise of happiness which they hold out is an illusion.

It is the destiny of mankind to work in order to live. Before the young married couple, especially in the modern world, stretches the prospect of long years of unremitting toil. There is the formidable undertaking of providing, equipping, and maintaining a home; and there is the high endeavour of raising a family. Not till they have reached middle life, if then, can the average couple hope for any considerable period of respite.

This need be no cause for discouragement. Young bodies and stout hearts thrive on tasks which test skill and endurance. Many elderly married couples, looking back over their span of life, have given it as their considered judgement that the happiest years of all were the years of toil and struggle and sacrifice during which they were establishing a home and bringing up their children. There are few deeper satisfactions than that which comes from doing a worthwhile job and doing it well.

A man may work because he takes a creative pride in what he is doing. He may work in order to get on, to fulfil his ambition to gain wealth or achieve recognition. But the best incentive of all lies in his desire to work so that his wife and family may be provided for. The link between a man's work and his home is close and deeply significant. He works in order that, first and foremost, he may bring the fruit of his labour and lay it as an offering at the feet of those whom he loves most dearly.

The wife who understands this will give her husband continuous encouragement by making the home a source of happiness and pride to him. He in turn will recognize that her creative activity in the home is just as important as his vocation, just as much a part of the world's work. Women have too often been discouraged by the way in which their task as home-makers has been undervalued. It is in fact the most important work of all, since not much of the rest of the world's work would continue to be done for long if home life ceased.

In modern times, however, the traditional distinction between man's work and woman's work has become blurred. Vast social and economic changes have created conditions in which all the work a man can do will not earn enough for his family's needs. At the same time, fortunately, doors of opportunity have opened for the woman, so that she is able to share directly in providing for the family. This has produced a situation in which a new tradition is arising, so that husband and wife will share the work both outside the home and within it. Though this calls for difficult adjustment in some cases, the principle is potentially sound. It provides the woman with a fuller opportunity for participating in the wider life of society, while the man is able to share more intimately in the tasks of home-making and in the care of his children. Rightly used, this opens up the way for men and women to achieve full co-operation, as equal partners, in every part of the world's life. When the way is hard and the adjustments difficult, it is encouraging to remember that the husbands and wives of today are pioneering the application of a great and important principle which has never before been put fully into practice.

PRAYER

May we so value our homes and loved ones, O God, that for their sakes no toil will seem too hard, no sacrifice too great, no offering too costly. As husband and wife, may we discover that because we love each other we can work the better, and because we work together we can love more truly. Amen.

4. Church Loyalty

And Joshua said, As for me and my house, we will serve the Lord. And the people answered and said, God forbid that we should forsake the Lord; for he it is that brought us and our fathers up out of the land of Egypt, and preserved us in all the way wherein we went.

JOSHUA 24[15, 16, 17]

The indestructible foundation of an ideal marriage is faith in God. Otherwise, in the larger as in the smaller world, the world of the man and that of the woman are no longer the same. When the natural ardour is extinguished, differences of temperament, education, and culture, built on the strong foundation of sexual differences, grow into mental separation. . . . It is otherwise when a common aim which is more than earthly unites them, when access to the eternal home stands open; when there is common prayer for forgiveness and grace; and faith in the one eternally true love of God, which makes all human love a symbol of its power.

THEODOR VON HAERING—*The Ethics of the Christian Life*

We express our purpose to enter into a life-long union of mutual faithfulness and devotion;

We recognize that marriage can be permanently happy and en-riching only through the cultivation of those qualities of self-control, forbearance and unselfish love which religious ideals can help to create;

And, therefore, for our own sakes and for the sake of the home which we hope to establish, we will seek to associate ourselves for worship and fellowship with some Christian church in the community where we reside.

(Statement signed by couples married at Grace Episcopal Church, New York.)

WHEN two married people share the same faith, and have a sense of spiritual unity, it is natural for them to want to express this experience by meeting regularly for worship with other like-minded people. By sharing their own personal religion with others they are better able to sustain and increase their faith than if they kept it to themselves. Belonging to the wider fellowship gives them also the security of an anchorage. When their faith is strong, they can help to strengthen others. When their faith is weak, others can help to strengthen them.

We tend to think of the Church as an institution, and we are justified in doing so. But the real continuing life of the Church is made possible only because it is a fellowship of Christian families. It is such families, generating a spirit of loyalty and devotion to Christ, and transmitting that spirit to the children in their midst, who have made possible the transition of the faith from one generation to another.

Our acceptance, as married couples, of church loyalty signifies our taking of the torch from those who bore it in the past and our passing it on to those who will bear it in the future. We belong to a Christian church because we believe that the world is the better and sweeter because of the Christian interpretation of truth and the Christian way of life. Week by week, as we attend worship, we renew our allegiance to that truth and seek to learn better how to live that life.

It is important to see clearly that the real meaning of our association with the Church is that it is an act of loyalty. It is pleasant for us if we like the church building and enjoy the sermons of the preacher and consider the music good. But these are not the reasons why we attend. We do not go to church to be entertained. We go because we do not desire Christianity, and all that it stands for, to perish from the earth; and that is exactly what could happen, in the course of a generation, if we as a married couple stopped going to church and everyone else followed our example.

Much the best way to fulfil your church loyalty is to make a clear-cut decision that you will attend worship together regularly every Sunday. To go now and then, in an erratic way, is ultimately harder than to go always. Decide that this is an appointment which is going to be kept with unfailing regularity. Such a decision makes the issue clear to your friends; and it sets an example to your children which they will follow without question. From such regular weekly attendance at worship all the other church loyalties will naturally spring. Plant your anchor firmly by binding this decision upon yourselves, and you will never be able to drift into forgetfulness of your duties and privileges as Christians.

When husband and wife come from different denominational backgrounds, or when one partner is indifferent about church attendance, it may be difficult to arrive at a common mind about church loyalty. Yet it is very important to be able to do so. When married couples cannot worship together, they deny themselves one of life's most satisfying experiences; and they present their children with a dilemma. Even if costly concessions have to be made, it is worth a great deal to be able to belong to the same church. Families which can be completely united about their church loyalty generally find that they can reach unity about other important issues.

PRAYER

We thank Thee, O God, that we are free to worship as we will. Grant that we may not abuse this freedom by neglect of the means of grace. Help us, as a token of our love and unity, to join in a

steadfast resolve that we will regularly fulfil the duties, and avail our-
selves of the privileges, of our faith. Amen.

5. *The Task of Parenthood*

The virtuous woman openeth her mouth with wisdom: and the law
of kindness is on her tongue. Her children rise up, and call her blessed.

PROVERBS 31[26, 28]

And ye fathers, provoke not your children to wrath.

EPHESIANS 6[4]

The child whose parents are fond of him accepts their affection as a
law of nature. He does not think very much about it, although
it is of great importance to his happiness. He thinks about the world,
about the adventures that come his way and the more marvellous
adventures that will come his way when he is grown up. But behind
all these external interests there is the feeling that he will be protected
from disaster by parental affection.

BERTRAND RUSSELL—*The Conquest of Happiness*

You may give them your love but not your thoughts,
For they have their own thoughts.
You may house their bodies but not their souls,
For their souls dwell in the house of tomorrow.
You may strive to be like them, but seek not to make them like you;
For life goes not backward nor tarries with yesterday.

KAHLIL GIBRAN—*The Prophet*

THE Hebrews believed that a man gains immortality, not so
much through individual survival after death, as in passing on
his essential self to his children. Most parents at some time or
other experience a sense of wonder, and a glow of satisfaction,
as they contemplate the idea of their own continuing life
through the sons and daughters whom they have brought into
the world.

   Yet it is an idea which has its dangers. If we consider our children as a continuation of our own life, we shall naturally want them to adopt our views and attitudes. This can easily result in a desire to realize our own ambitions (especially our unfulfilled ambitions) through them, and mould them into successful embodiments of what their parents strove to be. A child made to feel this kind of compulsion may suffer deeply and fail miserably.

As a matter of fact, it is not true that a child is merely the propagation of his parent's personality. The study of genetics has shown us that it is more true to say that both parents and child have dipped into the same family stock for the materials out of which they must fashion their lives. It does not follow that they have both drawn from the source the same equipment. They may in fact be very different types of persons.

This scientific truth guides us towards a right Christian approach to parenthood. Our children do not belong to us; neither are they replicas of us. They are unique individuals, whose right to be themselves must not be violated. It has been our privilege to create them. Yet we had no power to decide just what we were creating. That, mercifully, was not in our hands. At birth, we had to take them for what they were. They came to us as a sacred trust—the most sacred trust, surely, that men and women can receive.

What, then, is the task of parenthood? We sometimes speak of moulding our children. That is a word which can convey the wrong impression. We must not assume as much power as that. If we try to do so, we shall fail. Our task is to accept our children for what they are; to love them; to care for them; and to strive to surround them, as they grow up, with wholesome and good influences. Beyond that we have no right to go.

If we are to fulfil this task aright, we must guard our motives. Our love must be free from possessiveness. Our service must be given without any expectation of reward. We must not seek to glorify ourselves in the achievements of our children, nor shrink from sharing the humiliation of their failures because our pride is injured. Our discipline must not be the expression of our annoyance or of our desire to keep them dependent upon us, but a framework for their own achievement of self-discipline.

Clearly it is not easy to be a good parent. We shall need all the knowledge we can gain. We shall need a great deal of patience, a great deal of restraint. Above all, we shall need a great deal of love. All the overflow of love from the happiest married couple is not too much for the needs of their children. It is for this reason that the real key to successful parenthood is successful marriage.

The duties of parents are arduous. The rearing of a family is no side-line. It is a major undertaking. But where the task is faithfully accomplished, the duty is lost in the joy. There are few fulfilments to be compared with the gladness of those whose children say to them 'Well done!'

PRAYER

O Thou who, in showing men the likeness of heaven on earth, didst set a child in the midst; grant that in our love for our children there may always be mingled reverence. Grant us, in the responsible task of parenthood, a liberal share of wisdom, of devotion, and of humility. Amen.

6. Family Relationships

A father of the fatherless, and a judge of the widows, is God in his holy habitation. He setteth the solitary in families.

PSALM 68[5, 6]

To be happy at home is the ultimate result of all ambition; the end to which every enterprise and labour tends, and of which every desire promotes the prosecution.

SAMUEL JOHNSON—*The Rambler*

The family thus becomes the true theatre of goodness, because nowhere else can the identification of my interest with the interest of
others be either so complete or so natural.

W. F. LOFTHOUSE—*Ethics and the Family*

A married couple who love their home, their family, and their
friends, create a charmed circle and make a warmth which radiates all
it touches. To this sort of home, be it rich or poor in material things,
the children return at every opportunity; and from it they go out into
the world to start other homes of the same type, homes which are
built on the lasting love that husband and wife feel for each other.

MARY MACAULAY—*The Art of Marriage*

WITHIN a family most of us spend the greater part of our lives.
First it is our parental homes. Then, after a period of detach-
ment, we found new homes of our own. No art contributes
more to the sum total of human happiness than the art of
successful family living. Nothing causes more widespread
distress than the failure of families to live together in harmony.

The nucleus of the normal family is the marriage relationship of the parents. The quality of this affects, more decisively
than any other factor, the quality of the life of the home. You
cannot build a good house on bad foundations; and you cannot
fashion a harmonious family life out of a marriage torn by
conflict and maladjustment. Not for your own sakes alone is
it worth striving earnestly to make your marriage a success.
The happiness of all who share your home is equally at stake.

Mutual affection between husband and wife will be to the
family what the heating system is to a house. It will maintain
the relationship of all the family members in a pleasant and
comfortable atmosphere. That does not mean, however, that
the peace of the family will never be disturbed. Striving to
maintain a superficial peace may actually create a less happy
home than allowing hostility, when it arises, to express itself
and dissolve away. The point is that a family in which there is
true affection can meet disturbances of this kind without

suffering harm. It is not the absence of problems which marks the truly happy family, but the confident assurance that relationships in the home are basically so sound that they can deal with any problems which may arise.

Members of a family must learn not only to understand and to accept each other, but also to co-operate with each other in work and in play. This means that the life of a home must be based on law and order. A family, like a city or a country, must be efficiently organized if its life is to run smoothly and sweetly. Dr. Joseph Folsom has even suggested that families would achieve greater harmony if they drew up some kind of constitution to define the rights and duties of the various members. Whether it is put into writing or not, a family needs a code of agreed rules and principles. The only alternatives to this are a dictatorship, where one individual runs the lives of all the others; or a state of anarchy where every member does what is right in his own eyes.

The rules on which a home is run need, however, to be flexible. They must allow for the fact that the family is not a static institution, but a dynamic one in which the members are continually growing and changing. Probably the best way to meet this need is to make major decisions only after discussion in some kind of family council. It need not be a formal affair, and all the members need not be vested with equal authority. But the practice of allowing free discussion of all important issues goes a long way toward preventing resentment and rebellion and forging the family into a loyally co-operating group.

Good family relationships produce happy people inside the home, and help to make a happier world outside it.

PRAYER

O Lord, who hast planted in the hearts of men a deep love of home, and a great yearning for domestic happiness; grant us the steady resolution to create in our family life a quality and richness which shall bind us one to another in mutual gratitude, affection, and loyalty. Amen.

7. *The Christian Home*

And when Jesus came, he looked up, and said unto him, Zacchaeus, make haste, and come down; for today I must abide at thy house. And he made haste, and came down, and received him joyfully.

LUKE 19^{5, 6}

All genuine family life finds itself in the ideals of Christ. The true function of religion is to inspire reverence and eager love for those ideals, and to uphold them as the august will of God and the rapturous joy of man.

W. F. LOFTHOUSE—*Ethics and the Family*

The family is a little Church, a microcosm of the Body of Christ, and must manifest by its fellowship the church-like quality of its life.

DERRICK SHERWIN BAILEY—*The Mystery of Love and Marriage*

The sacred fire of domestic love, kindled from the altar of divine love, shall be carried far and wide into the world of human life, and shall create everywhere the light and warmth of home.

BISHOP HENSLEY HENSON—*Christian Marriage*

ALL good home life tends inevitably towards the practice of the Christian virtues. Indeed, it is only in terms of those virtues that family living can be successful at all. Every truly happy home, therefore, whether it professes to be a Christian home or not, is Christian in spirit.

The distinctive mark of a Christian home is that it is Christian both in its spirit and in its profession. It is necessary that it should be both of these. Christian virtues, as we have seen, can be cultivated by people who do not acknowledge the

Christian faith. It is equally true that people may profess and call themselves Christians who have not the spirit of Christ. It is a sad state of affairs indeed when a home which calls itself Christian does not manifest the fruits of Christian living.

A home which calls itself Christian will acknowledge its allegiance to Christ. This it will do first by worship. The family members will unite with other Christians in the corporate worship of the Church. They will also find their own way, within the home, of acknowledging God. The parents will seek to cultivate their personal devotional life, and will encourage the children to do likewise. They may join in some regular act of devotion as a family group, such as the saying of grace before meals or uniting in family prayers. Such devotional practices will achieve their purpose if participation in them is united and spontaneous. If they become forced or formal, however, they may degenerate into meaningless acts devoid of any religious significance. Each Christian family must be free to discover its own ways of expressing its religious life, and to avoid adopting stereotyped patterns which may be unsuited to it.

The Christian family will not only be a worshipping community, but also a serving community. The parents will try to encourage, by their example, the principle of helping others, and sharing family joys and privileges with those less fortunate. The Christian home is not self-contained and wrapped up in itself. It is imbued with a sense of mission. In its relations with the community to which it belongs it will seek always to give more than it takes, to espouse every good cause, to stand ready to meet human need. Thus the children of Christian parents come to think of their home not as a place provided exclusively for their own enjoyment, but rather as one where they are learning to find their happiness in serving others.

Through its worship and its service, the Christian home bears witness to the faith to which it is dedicated. It does not set out deliberately to provide an example to others; for that would be to judge others and to imply that it was superior to them. Yet inevitably the Christian home *does* set an example. Insofar as it achieves the qualities of a truly Christian community, it is a little colony of the Kingdom of Heaven. It is a working unit which demonstrates what all community life would be like in a Christian world.

The Christian home is, in fact, by far the most powerful evangelizing agency in the world. Its evangelism, however, is not aggressive; it is persuasive. It proclaims its message not by words, but by deeds. It does not tell others what they should be; it shows them what they could be. By their gracious influence, Christian homes win more converts than all the preachers put together. Give us enough of them, and the world would soon be a Christian world; for the world's life rises to higher levels only as its homes do so.

PRAYER

O God, whose desire is that all the peoples of the world should be one human family, living together in harmony and peace; grant that our home, by its worship and its witness, may help to hasten the day when Thy will shall be done on earth as it is in heaven. Amen.

APPENDIX

Books Recommended for Further Reading

There are many books on marriage. A very long list would only confuse the ordinary reader. I have therefore confined this list to twelve volumes. I have chosen them, first, because they are fairly simple and easy to read; second, because they are readily available. They cover various aspects of marriage, and most of them contain lists of other books for further reading.

Clatworthy, Nancy M., and Folkman, Jerome D., *Marriage Has Many Faces*. Charles E. Merrill Publishing Company, 1970.
This is a college text, and the biggest book on our list. It covers many aspects of marriage, but is not difficult to read.

Clinebell, Howard J., Jr., and Charlotte H., *The Intimate Marriage*. Harper & Row, Publishers, Inc., 1970.
This is a very creative book about developing communication and interaction in marriage, written by two very experienced marriage counselors.

Eichenlaub, John E., *The Marriage Art*. Dell Publishing Company, Inc., 1969.
A step-by-step guide to sexual intercourse suitable for the about-to-be-married, written by a physician who has done a great deal of counseling with married couples.

Hamilton, Eleanor, *Partners in Love: The Modern Bride Book of Sex and Marriage,* Rev. Ed. A. S. Barnes & Company, Inc., 1968.
An experienced marriage counselor talks about the intimate life of the married couple.

Mace, David R., *Getting Ready for Marriage*. Abingdon Press, 1972.
Addressed directly to the couple approaching marriage, this book attempts to provide as nearly as possible a series of premarital counseling sessions.

—— *Success in Marriage.* Abingdon Press, 1958.
This is a book about the many aspects of marriage, and how the partners should handle them in order to achieve a good relationship.

McGinnis, Tom, *Your First Year of Marriage.* Doubleday & Company, Inc., 1967.
A book about the adjustments a couple will need to make in their first year, written by a former President of the American Association of Marriage and Family Counselors.

Otto, Herbert A., *More Joy in Your Marriage.* Hawthorn Books, Inc., 1969.
This unusual book is full of practical suggestions about ways in which couples can increase their awareness and understanding of themselves and of each other.

Riker, Audrey P., *et al, Married Life.* Chas. A. Bennett Co., Inc., 1970.
This is a big book of 543 pages, and covers everything from the planning of the wedding to the personal relationships of the couple, and the many aspects of their life together.

Rodenmayer, Robert N., *I, John, Take Thee, Mary.* The Seabury Press, Inc., 1964.
A book written specially, from a Christian point of view, for couples preparing for marriage, dealing with most of the matters that will concern them.

Shedd, Charlie W., *Letters to Karen: On Keeping Love in Marriage.* Abingdon Press, 1965.
A book of letters from a father to his daughter, who is about to be married.

—— *Letters to Phillip: On How to Treat a Woman.* Doubleday & Company, Inc., 1968.
The same father now writes to his son, as he in turn approaches marriage.